GET BY IN
GERMAN

A QUICK BEGINNER'S COURSE FOR
HOLIDAYMAKERS AND BUSINESS PEOPLE

JOACHIM KOTHE

BBC BOOKS

Published by BBC Books
an imprint of BBC Worldwide Publishing.
BBC Worldwide Ltd.
Woodlands
80 Wood Lane,
London W12 0TT

First published 1992
© Joachim Kothe 1992

Reprinted 1992 (twice), 1993 (twice), 1994
This edition published in 1995
Reprinted 1995, 1996 (twice)

Edited by Iris Sprankling

The moral right of the author has been asserted

ISBN 0 563 399589

Designed by Peter Bridgewater
Map and Illustrations by Lorraine Harrison
Cover designed by Peter Bridgewater
and Annie Moss

Set in Great Britain by
Central Southern Typesetters, Eastbourne
Printed in England by Clays Ltd, St Ives plc

Cover printed by Clays Ltd, St Ives plc

Exclusive U.S. Distributor of the Get By in Series Pack

Ambrose Video Publishing, Inc.
1290 Avenue of the Americas
Suite 2245
New York,
N.Y. 10104

CONTENTS

INTRODUCTION

The new *Get by in German* is a quick beginners' course for anyone planning to visit Germany or any German-speaking country on business or for pleasure. It consists of two audio-cassettes and this book. A videocassette, including further conversations and interviews, is also available, accompanied by a handbook.

Get by in German will not equip you to hold lengthy conversations in German, but it **will** help you to:

● Make yourself understood in everyday situations, such as ordering a drink, finding your way about, shopping, making a phone call, and so on
● Understand what people may say to you
● Get used to the sounds and patterns of German, a good foundation should you wish to take your German further
● Make new friends and get more out of your trip by 'having a go' at the language.

Get by in German is based on real-life conversations specially recorded in Hamburg in northern Germany, so you get used to hearing authentic German right from the start.

THE AUDIOCASSETTES

The cassettes:

● Contain the conversations reproduced in this book
● Explain the language you need to speak and understand in each situation
● Give you plenty of opportunities to repeat words and expressions aloud, answer simple questions and take part in conversations like those you might have abroad
● Allow you to study at your own pace.

THE BOOK

This book includes:

● Key words and phrases used in each unit

- Transcripts of the recorded conversations
- Further word lists for each unit
- Brief explanations of language points
- Exercises to help you practise your skills
- Basic information and tips about life in Germany
- Final test to see if you can *Get by*
- Reference section containing a simple guide to German pronunciation (you can hear this at the end of the second cassette) and useful language notes
- Complete list of words used in the course.

TO MAKE THE MOST OF THE COURSE

- First of all look through the unit in the book to give yourself an idea of what to expect. Then listen to the cassette. There are pauses for you to practise pronunciation, answer questions and take part in conversations. Join in aloud and, if you don't get it quite right the first time, wind back the cassette and listen again. If the pause isn't long enough, you can always use the pause button on your cassette player to extend it. Go through the exercises several times until you can do them with no mistakes.
- When you've worked through the cassette, go back to the book and read the conversation transcripts again, revise the explanations and try the exercises.
- Lastly, play the cassettes as often as possible – in the car, working around the house, or on your personal cassette player when shopping or walking the dog.
- One final suggestion: if you're learning with someone else, take advantage of the opportunity to 'act out' the dialogues, repeating them again and again until you can do them without the book. As you get more confident, you can try making variations of your own.

We hope you enjoy *Get by in German*. And wherever you go in the future in the German-speaking world . . . *Gute Reise und viel Spaß!*

1 MEETING PEOPLE

KEY WORDS AND PHRASES

HELLOS AND GOODBYES

guten Morgen	good morning
guten Tag	good morning, good afternoon (*lit.* good day)
guten Abend	good evening
hallo	hello
(auf) Wiedersehen	(good)bye
tschüs	cheers, cheerio, 'bye
wie geht's? **wie geht es Ihnen?**	how are you?
danke, gut	fine, thanks

BREAKING THE ICE

wie heißen Sie?	what's your name?
woher kommen Sie?	where are you from?
ich komme/bin aus . . .	I'm from . . .
das ist . . .	this is . . .

ORDERING DRINKS

Herr Ober!	waiter!
ein Kännchen Tee	a pot of tea
eine Cola	a coke
noch zwei Bier	two more beers

bitte	please
danke	thank you

CONVERSATIONS

The following conversations are included on the cassette.
Listen to them carefully. The important words and phrases
are listed above, but look up any other words you don't
understand in the word list following the conversations. The
Explanations section will help you with language points to be
found in the conversations.

OUT AND ABOUT IN HAMBURG

Hello. How are you?

FR. HARRINGTON Guten Tag, Herr Hinze.

HERR HINZE Oh, hallo, Frau Harrington. Wie geht es
Ihnen?

FR. HARRINGTON Ach ja, ganz gut. Und Ihnen?

HERR HINZE Danke, gut.

Good morning. Fine, thanks. And you?

FRAU PAGITZ Guten Morgen, Frau Peters.

FRAU PETERS 'n Morgen, Frau Pagitz.

FRAU PAGITZ Wie geht's?

FRAU PETERS Danke, gut. Und Ihnen?

FRAU PAGITZ Och, danke. Es geht.

VISITING FRAU PETERS

Good evening. This is Frau Pagitz.

FRAU PETERS *(answering the doorbell)* Ach, Herr Dr.
Göttsch. Guten Abend.

DR. GÖTTSCH	Guten Abend, Frau Peters. Darf ich vorstellen, das ist Frau Pagitz.
FRAU PAGITZ	Guten Abend, Frau Peters.
FRAU PETERS	Guten Abend, Frau Pagitz. Kommen Sie doch bitte rein.

Goodbye!

HAMBURGER	Auf Wiedersehen! Wiedersehen! Wiederschauen! Tschüs!

Are you from Hamburg? No, I'm from Speyer.

FRAU PAGITZ	Frau Peters, sind Sie aus Hamburg?
FRAU PETERS	Nein, ich bin nicht aus Hamburg. Ich komme aus Speyer. Das liegt in Rheinland-Pfalz.

What's your name? Where are you from?

FRAU PAGITZ	Wie heißen Sie, bitte?
FRAU BEHRENS	Barbara Behrens.
FRAU PAGITZ	Sind Sie aus Hamburg, Frau Behrens?
FRAU BEHRENS	Nein, ich bin Engländerin.
FRAU PAGITZ	Ach, Sie sind Engländerin!
FRAU BEHRENS	Ja.
FRAU PAGITZ	Woher kommen Sie?
FRAU BEHRENS	Ich komme aus Bristol.

I'm a Hamburger.

FRAU PAGITZ	Sind Sie aus Hamburg?
DR. GÖTTSCH	Ja, ich bin Hamburger.

REFRESHMENTS

In the Alsterpavillon. Waiter! A pot of tea, please. With lemon.

FRAU EVRAHR	Herr Ober!

OBER	Ja, bitte schön?
FRAU EVRAHR	Bitte, ein Kännchen Tee.
OBER	Möchten Sie den Tee mit Sahne oder Zitrone?
FRAU EVRAHR	Gern mit Zitrone.
OBER	Gerne.

In the pub Die Glocke (The Bell).
A coke, a mineral water and a wine. A white one.

FR. HARRINGTON	Herr Ober!
OBER	Ja, bitte?
FR. HARRINGTON	Eine Cola, ein Mineralwasser und ein' Wein, bitte.
OBER	Möchten Sie einen roten oden einen weißen Wein?
FR. HARRINGTON	Einen weißen, bitte.
OBER	Wird gemacht!

Two beers, please. Large ones.

GAST	Herr Ober! Zwei Bier, bitte.
OBER	Große oder kleine?
GAST	Zwei große, bitte.

Two more beers. And two more schnaps as well.

GAST	Herr Ober!
OBER	Ja, bitte?
GAST	Bringen Sie noch zwei Bier, bitte.
OBER	Ja, gerne.
GAST	Und noch zwei Kurze dazu.
OBER	Ist in Ordnung.

Six-year-old Berthe counts up to ten.

BERTHE	Eins, zwei, drei, vier, fünf, sechs, sieben, acht, neun, zehn.
FR. HARRINGTON	Noch einmal, ein kleines bißchen langsamer, bitte . . .

BERTHE Eins, zwei, drei, vier, fünf, sechs, sieben, acht, neun, zehn.

FR. HARRINGTON Schön hast du das gemacht, Berthe.

WORD LIST

ganz gut	quite well
und Ihnen?	and you?
es geht	not too bad
darf ich vorstellen . . . ?	may I introduce . . . ?
kommen Sie rein	come in
das liegt in . . .	that's (situated) in . . .
bitte schön?	yes, please?
möchten Sie . . . ?	would you like . . . ?
mit Sahne oder Zitrone?	with cream or lemon?
einen roten oder einen weißen?	a red one or a white one?
wird gemacht	right away
der Gast	guest
große oder kleine?	large or small?
bringen Sie mir . . .	bring me . . .
zwei Kurze	two 'shorts'
dazu	as well
noch einmal	once again
ein bißchen langsamer	a bit more slowly
schön hast du das gemacht	you did that (very) nicely

EXPLANATIONS

HELLO

Between getting up and about midday: *guten Morgen!*
All day until 5 or 6 p.m.: *guten Tag!*
In the evening: *guten Abend!*
Informally to people you know: *hallo!*

In practice the *guten* is often swallowed, so you'll hear: *'n Morgen! 'n Tag! 'n Abend!*

Depending on which part of Germany you're in, you may come across regional variations like the north German *Moin! ('n Morgen!)* and *Tach! ('n Tag)*. Especially in southern Germany and Austria, people say: *grüß Gott! (lit.* 'greet God!').

GOODBYE

Auf Wiedersehen! (or *Wiedersehen!*) and *auf Wiederschauen!* (or *Wiederschauen!*) mean literally 'until we see each other again'. More casually you can say *tschüs!*, which is like 'cheers!', 'cheerio!' or ''bye!'.

HOW ARE YOU?

To find out ask: *wie geht es Ihnen?* or *wie geht's?*
Mostly you can answer: *danke, gut* (fine, thanks) or: *danke, es geht* (not too bad, thanks).
If you really are under the weather, say: *danke, nicht gut* (not very well). In which case you might get the reply: *gute Besserung!* (get well soon!)

INTRODUCTIONS

To introduce someone else, start with:
das ist . . . this is . . .
You'd say:
das ist | *Herr/Frau/Fräulein* . . .
| Mr/Mrs/Miss . . .
| *Herr Doktor/Frau Doktor* . . .
Like Dr. Göttsch, you can put *darf ich vorstellen?* (may I introduce?) in front:
Darf ich vorstellen? Das ist Frau Pagitz.

To introduce yourself:
ich bin . . . I'm . . .
or: *ich heiße . . .* my name's . . .
If you haven't been introduced, you could ask:
wie heißen Sie, bitte? what's your name, please?

WHERE ARE YOU FROM?

To find out, ask:
sind Sie aus . . . ? are you from . . . ?
woher kommen Sie? where do you come from?
To answer, you can say:
ja/nein yes/no
ich komme/bin (nicht) aus . . . I'm (not) from . . .

NATIONALITIES

Are you Scottish? Welsh? American? Irish? English? Then, if
you're a man, say:
ich bin . . . Schotte, Waliser, Amerikaner, Ire, Engländer
If you're a woman, the nationality usually ends with *-in:*
ich bin . . . Schottin, Waliserin, Amerikanerin, Irin, Engländerin

ORDERING DRINKS

Just say what you want, and add 'please':

ein Kännchen Tee,
ein Wein,
noch zwei Bier,   *bitte*
eine Cola,

You may be offered a choice:
mit Sahne oder Zitrone?
einen roten oder einen weißen?
große oder kleine?
Then simply repeat the option you'd like:
große, bitte

HAMBURGER OR *HAMBURGER*?

It's not usually difficult to tell whether people are talking about fast food or an inhabitant of Hamburg!

What do you suppose a resident of Frankfurt is called? And what did President Kennedy say in Berlin?

'THE' AND 'A'

German has three kinds of nouns: masculine (m.), feminine (f.) and neuter (n.). The words you use for 'the' and 'a' vary accordingly:

	MASCULINE	FEMININE	NEUTER
the	**der** *Tag*	**die** *Dame*	**das** *Bier*
a	**ein** *Tag*	**eine** *Dame*	**ein** *Bier*

Unfortunately there's not much logic about which words are which gender. It's best to learn them as you go along. Don't worry if you get it wrong. You'll still be understood.

'YOU' AND 'I'

In this chapter you've met several verbs. With *ich* (I) the ending is usually *-e* and with *Sie* (you) it's usually *-en:*

	gehen	*kommen*	*heißen*	*bringen*
	to go	to come	to be called	to bring
ich:	*gehe*	*komme*	*heiße*	*bringe*
Sie:	*gehen*	*kommen*	*heißen*	*bringen*

But there's an important exception:
sein (to be):   *ich bin   Sie sind*

CAPITAL LETTERS

One peculiarity of German is that you write nouns with a capital letter: *das Bier, der Abend*. *Sie* and *Ihnen* also have a capital when they mean 'you':
sind Sie aus Hamburg?
wie geht es Ihnen?

THE *UMLAUT* AND *ß*

German has four letters that don't exist in any other language: *ä; ö; ü*; and *ß*. The two dots over the vowels, called an *Umlaut*, change the vowels' sound. The ß stands for 'ss'.
grüß Gott!   *bitte schön*
ein Kännchen Tee   große oder kleine?

NUMBERS 1–10

eins, zwei, drei, vier, fünf, sechs, sieben, acht, neun, zehn

If you don't understand them (or anything else!) the first time, get them repeated: *noch einmal, bitte*   more slowly: *langsamer!*

EXERCISES

HELLO AND GOODBYE

1a You come into your hotel at 2 p.m. How do you greet the porter?
 b You return at 7 p.m. What do you say?
 c You meet your friend Dieter. Say hello.
 d And how do you say goodbye to him?

HOW ARE YOU?

2 You meet Herr Meier in the street. How does your conversation go?

SIE	_____ .
HERR MEIER	Ach, hallo! Wie geht's?
SIE	_____
	und _____ ?
HERR MEIER	_____ , auch _____ . (*auch* = also)

WHERE ARE YOU FROM?

3 You get into conversation with a passenger on the train. What do you say?

PASSAGIER	Sind Sie aus Holland?
SIE	(No, you're a Scot.)
PASSAGIER	Sind Sie aus Edinburgh?
SIE	(From Edinburgh? No, you're *not* from Edinburgh!)
PASSAGIER	Woher kommen Sie denn?
SIE	(You're from Glasgow.)

ORDERING DRINKS

4 In a pub you order a small beer for yourself and then a whisky on-the-rocks for your friend:

SIE	_____ !
OBER	Ja, bitte schön?
SIE	_____ .
OBER	Ein großes oder ein kleines?
SIE	_____ . Und _____ .
OBER	Möchten Sie den Whisky mit Eis oder mit Wasser?
SIE	_____ .
OBER	Gerne.

MORE DRINKS

5 You've invited a German friend and his daughter to the Café Reckers. What do you say?

SIE	(Would you like coffee?)
FREUND	Nein. Ich nehme Tee.
SIE	(With lemon or milk?)
FREUND	Mit Milch, bitte. Und Sie? Möchten Sie auch Tee?
SIE	(No, I'd like coffee.)
TOCHTER	Und ich möchte . . .
SIE	(Would you like tea?)
TOCHTER	Nein, Tee nicht.
SIE	(Would you like hot chocolate?)
TOCHTER	Oh ja, bitte.
SIE	(A small or large cup?)
TOCHTER	Eine große Tasse, bitte.
SIE	(Call the waiter.)
OBER	Ja, bitte?
SIE	(Order a pot of tea, a pot of coffee and a large cup of hot chocolate.)
OBER	Ja, gerne.

Café Reckers

HEISSE GETRÄNKE

Kaffee (Kännchen) 5,85 DM

Tee (Kännchen) mit Zitrone oder Milch 5,85 DM

Heiße Schokolade

(kleine Tasse) 2,75 DM

(große Tasse) 5,– DM

Irish Coffee 7,65 DM

WORTH KNOWING

SAYING HELLO

When you go into somewhere like a shop, restaurant or office, you generally say *guten Morgen/Tag/Abend!* and, when you leave, *auf Wiedersehen!* On a more personal level people usually shake hands when they say hello or goodbye. Sometimes, even at large gatherings, you go round and shake hands with everybody, introducing yourself where necessary. The same may happen at business meetings. With good friends you might exchange kisses.

FIRST NAME OR SURNAME?

In Germany it's not as common as in English-speaking countries to be on first-name terms straightaway, though this varies with the situation and the age group of the people. The best advice is to listen carefully to what the others do, then do the same. If in doubt, choose *Herr, Frau* or *Fräulein.* But be careful! Many unmarried women regard being called *Fräulein* as a form of discrimination, so if in doubt say *Frau.*

GETTING A DRINK

In Germany you'll find a large variety of snack bars (*der Imbiß*), pubs (*die Kneipe, die Gaststätte*), cafés (*das Café, die Konditorei*) and restaurants (*das Restaurant*). There are virtually no restrictions on opening hours and licensing laws are very liberal.

You go to an *Imbiß* for a quick stand-up snack or drink, usually tea, coffee, a soft drink or beer. In pubs you get every sort of drink, although usually only one or two kinds of beer are on draught. Especially in northern Germany, you often drink a 'short' (*ein Kurzer, ein Klarer*) alongside your beer.

Mostly this is a clear (*klar*) ice-cold *Schnaps* made from grain. It's supposed to warm up the stomach for the cold beer to come. On the other hand some would say that's just an excuse! Pubs don't always serve food, and if they do, there'll be a rather limited menu.

In cafés you'll find mainly coffee, tea, pastries and gateaux but alcoholic and soft drinks are also served, and some offer light snack-type meals as well. Warning: a pot of tea may be up to six times more expensive than in Britain! Service charge (*Bedienung*) and VAT (*Mehrwertsteuer*) are usually included in the price on the menu, but the waiter still expects a tip of up to 10% on top of the bill!

THE ALSTERPAVILLON

The Alster is a tributary of the river Elbe dammed up to form two huge lakes, one of them the *Binnenalster,* in the Hamburg city centre. The *Alsterpavillon,* built in 1799 by a French émigré, is a café and restaurant beautifully situated on the *Binnenalster* and a favourite rendezvous for locals and tourists alike.

DRINKS

Most alcoholic drinks are the same in German as in English (*Whisky, Gin, Sherry,* etc.), but here are some others you might like to try:·

Limonade	lemonade
Sprudel	lemonade (n. Ger.); mineral water (s. Ger.)
Alsterwasser (n. Ger.)	shandy
Radler (s. Ger.)	shandy
Moorwasser	lemonade with coke
Apfelsaft	apple juice
Orangensaft	orange juice

Traubensaft	grape juice
(heiße) Schokolade	(hot) chocolate
Malzbier	dark, sweet beer with very little alcohol
Bier alkoholfrei	low-alcohol beer★

★Low-alcohol beer may be declared alcohol-free (*alkoholfrei*) in Germany but it still contains a small percentage of alcohol. In addition you can get 'light' beers which usually have about half the alcohol content of ordinary German beer.

2 SHOPPING

SAYING WHAT YOU WANT

ich hätte gern . . .	I'd like . . .
ich möchte . . .	
haben Sie . . . ?	have you . . . ?
das ist alles	that's all
200 Gramm (Käse)	200 grams (of cheese)
ein Pfund (Tomaten)	a pound (of tomatoes)
ein Kilo (Bananen)	a kilo (of bananas)
ein Paket (Schwarzbrot)	a packet (of rye bread)

THE SHOP ASSISTANT MAY ASK:

was darf ich Ihnen geben?	what would you like?
was kann ich für Sie tun?	may I help you?
was hätten Sie gern?	
was hätten Sie noch gerne?	
haben Sie sonst noch einen Wunsch?	would you like anything else?

PAYING

was macht das?	how much does that come to?

CONVERSATIONS

FOOD SHOPPING

200 grams of Dutch cheese, please. In a piece.

VERKÄUFERIN	Guten Tag.
FRAU EVRAHR	Guten Tag.
VERKÄUFERIN	Was darf ich Ihnen geben?
FRAU EVRAHR	Bitte zweihundert Gramm Holländer.
VERKÄUFERIN	Möchten Sie es im Stück oder geschnitten?
FRAU EVRAHR	Im Stück.
VERKÄUFERIN	Im Stück . . .
FRAU EVRAHR	Ja.
VERKÄUFERIN	Ja.

A pound of tomatoes, please. Nice ripe ones.

VERKÄUFERIN	Guten Abend. Was kann ich für Sie tun?
FRAU EVRAHR	Ein Pfund Tomaten, bitte.
VERKÄUFERIN	Gerne.
FRAU EVRAHR	Schön reife, bitte.
VERKÄUFERIN	*(weighs them)* Haben Sie sonst noch einen Wunsch?
FRAU EVRAHR	Ja, ein Kilo Bananen.
VERKÄUFERIN	Gerne.

Six rolls and a packet of rye bread.

FRAU ANTHES	Guten Tag. Was hätten Sie denn gerne?
FRAU EVRAHR	Sechs Brötchen, bitte.
FRAU ANTHES	Sechs Brötchen, ja . . . *(puts them in a bag)* Und was hätten Sie denn noch gerne?
FRAU EVRAHR	Schwarzbrot. Ein Paket Schwarzbrot.
FRAU ANTHES	Ein Paket Schwarzbrot . . . *(reaches down the packet)* Sonst noch einen Wunsch?
FRAU EVRAHR	Das ist alles.
FRAU ANTHES	Danke schön.

WINE AND ROSES

I'd like some roses. Seven yellow ones, please.

FRAU EVRAHR   Ich hätte gerne Rosen.

FRAU WITTROCK   Und welche Farbe darf es sein?

FRAU EVRAHR   Gelbe.

FRAU WITTROCK   Ja. Und wieviel?

FRAU EVRAHR   Sieben Stück.

FRAU WITTROCK   Gern.

A bottle of wine, please. Have you got a Moselle?

FR. HARRINGTON   Ich möchte gerne eine Flasche Wein.

HERR PLUSCHKE   Bitte schön, meine Dame. Möchten Sie einen Weißwein oder einen Rotwein?

FR. HARRINGTON   Einen Weißwein.

HERR PLUSCHKE   Weißwein.

FR. HARRINGTON   Haben Sie einen Mosel?

HERR PLUSCHKE   Hab' ich, natürlich. Ich habe hier zum Beispiel einen Marienburger Riesling für acht Mark fünfundneunzig.

FR. HARRINGTON   Das klingt gut. Den nehme ich.

HERR PLUSCHKE   Ja. Bitte schön.

POSTCARDS AND STAMPS

These two postcards, please. Have you got stamps?

FRAU EVRAHR   Guten Tag. Diese zwei Karten, bitte.

FRAU THEEL   Ja, danke schön. Das macht zwei Mark.

FRAU EVRAHR   Haben Sie Briefmarken?

FRAU THEEL   Tut mir leid. Hab' ich leider nicht.

How much is a postcard to Great Britain?

FRAU EVRAHR   Wieviel kostet eine Postkarte nach Großbritannien?

FRAU WEHLING   Sechzig Pfennig.

FRAU EVRAHR	Dann nehme ich sechs Briefmarken zu sechzig, bitte.
FRAU WEHLING	Sechs Briefmarken zu sechzig, gerne . . . *(handing her the stamps)* Bitte schön. Das macht drei Mark und sechzig, bitte.

PAYING

Frau Evrahr is paying for the roses. How much does that come to?

FRAU EVRAHR	Was macht das?
FRAU WITTROCK	Neun Mark und zehn.
FRAU EVRAHR	*(paying)* Zehn Mark.
FRAU WITTROCK	Danke schön. Und neunzig Pfennig zurück.
FRAU EVRAHR	Ja. Danke.

Paying for the rolls and rye bread.

FRAU EVRAHR	Und was macht das?
FRAU ANTHES	Das macht jetzt fünf Mark und fünfundneunzig.
FRAU EVRAHR	Gut.
FRAU ANTHES	Fünf Mark fünfundneunzig, und fünf *(giving the change)*.
FRAU EVRAHR	Danke sehr.

CASHING TRAVELLER'S CHEQUES

I'd like to cash some traveller's cheques.

HR. HASENJÄGER	Ich möchte gern Reiseschecks einlösen.
FRAU WITTKE	Ja, gerne. Wenn Sie dann hier bitte einmal unterschreiben würden.
HR. HASENJÄGER	Hier?
FRAU WITTKE	Ja.

WORD LIST

die Verkäuferin	shop assistant
im Stück oder geschnitten?	in a piece or sliced?
welche Farbe darf es sein?	which colour would you like?
wieviel?/wie viele?	how much?/how many?
meine Dame	madam
hab' ich	yes, I have
natürlich	of course
ich habe hier . . .	I have here . . .
zum Beispiel	for example
das klingt gut	that sounds good
den nehme ich	I'll take it
das macht	that's (that comes to)
tut mir leid	sorry
leider nicht	I'm afraid not
wieviel kostet . . . ?	how much does . . . cost?
dann nehme ich . . .	then I'll take . . .
zurück	change (*lit.* back)
jetzt	now
wenn Sie dann hier bitte einmal unterschreiben würden	if you'd just sign here then

EXPLANATIONS

SHOP TALK

Shop assistants have their own favourite ways of asking what you'd like:

was darf ich Ihnen geben?
was kann ich für Sie tun?
was hätten Sie denn gerne?
was darf es sein?
kann ich Ihnen helfen?

And, when they've served you with the first item, they'll probably ask, 'anything else?':
haben Sie sonst noch einen Wunsch?
sonst noch etwas?
darf es noch etwas sein?
was hätten Sie noch gerne?

You see that each of those questions contains the word *noch*. If you hear *noch,* you'll know they're asking if you want more.

To ask for what you want, name the item and add 'please':
sechs Brötchen, bitte
bitte, zweihundert Gramm Holländer
or you can start with 'I'd like':
ich hätte gerne Rosen
ich möchte gerne eine Flasche Wein
And to check if they've got something:
haben Sie Briefmarken?
haben Sie einen Mosel?

QUANTITIES

By law, prices for unpacked foods have to be given either per kilogram (1000g) or per 100g. Even on packed foods you'll always find the price for one kilogram to allow comparison. Very often you buy food by the pound, which in Germany means 500g or half a kilo:

a pound: *ein Pfund Tomaten*
a quarter: *ein Viertelpfund (125g) Holländer*
Or you might want:
a packet: *ein Paket Schwarzbrot*
a tin: *eine Dose (Büchse) Sardinen*
a carton: *eine Tüte Milch*

Remember that in German you don't need a word for 'of':

ein Kilo Äpfel   a kilo of apples
eine Flasche Wein   a bottle of wine

COLOURS

blau	blue	*grün*	green
braun	brown	*rot*	red
gelb	yellow	*schwarz*	black
grau	grey	*weiß*	white

SECHS STÜCK, BITTE

Stück means 'piece', but you can also use it to say how many of something you want:

wie viele Rosen?   *sieben Stück, bitte*
wie viele Brötchen?   *sechs Stück, bitte*
wie viele Postkarten?   *drei Stück, bitte*

MORE ABOUT NUMBERS

To understand prices you need to know numbers. There's a full list on page 00, but here are a few points to help you on the way:

- 11 and 12 are *elf* and *zwölf*
- The teens end with *-zehn* and the tens (except *dreißig*) with *-zig*:

4 *vier*	14 *vierzehn*	40 *vierzig*
5 *fünf*	15 *fünfzehn*	50 *fünfzig*

- From 20 on, Germans say 'one and twenty', 'two and twenty', etc.:

einundzwanzig, zweiundzwanzig, dreiundzwanzig, vierundzwanzig

- If you need to write them out, numbers are written as one word!

MONEY MATTERS

The *Deutsche Mark* (DM) or *die Mark* consists of 100 pfennigs (*der Pfennig*). Prices are spoken as they are in English:

£1.20:   one pound (and) twenty (pence)

1,20 DM: *eine Mark (und) zwanzig (Pfennige)*

But you'll notice that, when prices are written, there's a stop between the pounds and pence but a comma between the marks and pfennigs.

German currency comes in the following denominations:

Coins: 1 *Pfennig*, 2 *Pfennig*, 5 *Pfennig*, 10 *Pfennig*, 50 *Pfennig*, 1 *Mark*, 2 *Mark*, 5 *Mark*

Notes: 5 *Mark*, 10 *Mark*, 20 *Mark*, 50 *Mark*, 100 *Mark*, 200 *Mark*, 500 *Mark*, 1000 *Mark*.

EXERCISES

YOUR SHOPPING LIST

1 *Bitte schön?* On your shopping list are:

2 postcards

500g of Edam cheese *(Edamer)*

8 bread rolls

a packet of biscuits *(Kekse)*

5 roses

a bottle of red wine

a pound of apples *(Äpfel)*

a carton of milk

Ask for them as simply as possible.

2 *Was macht das?* How would you write these prices in figures?

zwei Mark siebenunddreißig

vierundzwanzig Mark elf

siebzehn Mark dreiundvierzig

AT THE DELICATESSEN

3 You are out shopping. Your first stop is at the delicatessen for 300g of Dutch cheese. What do you say to the assistant?

VERKÄUFERIN	Was kann ich für Sie tun?
SIE	_____.
VERKÄUFERIN	Im Stück oder geschnitten?
SIE	(You want it sliced.)
VERKÄUFERIN	Bitte sehr.
SIE	_____.

THE MARKET FRUIT STALL

Tomaten	kg 3,99 DM
Orangen	Stück 0,75 DM
Bananen	kg 2,70 DM
Äpfel	kg 2,80 DM
Kiwis	Stück 0,60 DM
Birnen	kg 2,95 DM

4 You go to the market. The fruit looks good so you decide to buy some. What do you say?

VERKÄUFER	Was darf ich Ihnen geben?
SIE	(1kg of tomatoes, please.)
VERKÄUFER	Gern. Sonst noch etwas?
SIE	(Yes, 500g of bananas.)
VERKÄUFER	Ja. Und sonst noch etwas?
SIE	(Has he got kiwi fruit?)
VERKÄUFER	Ja, wie viele möchten Sie denn?
SIE	(Eight, please.)
VERKÄUFER	So, bitte schön.

5 *Und was macht das?* Look at the stallholder's list to work out how much you have to pay.

AT THE POST OFFICE

6   You want to write home, so on to the post office (postcards you buy from a post office are blank and have a printed stamp). What do you say to the clerk?

BEAMTIN	Kann ich Ihnen helfen?
SIE	(How much is a letter, *der Brief,* to England?)
BEAMTIN	Eine Mark.
SIE	(You'd like three stamps, please.)
BEAMTIN	Bitte schön. Sonst noch etwas?
SIE	(Ask if she's got postcards.)
BEAMTIN	Ja, hab' ich. Wie viele möchten Sie denn?
SIE	(Four. Ask how much a postcard costs.)
BEAMTIN	60 Pfennig.
SIE	(How much does that come to, please?)
BEAMTIN	Drei Mark und zwei Mark vierzig, das sind fünf Mark vierzig.
SIE	(Hand her the money.)
BEAMTIN	Vielen Dank. Und vierundvierzig sechzig zurück. Auf Wiedersehen.
SIE	(Thank you and goodbye.)

7   You pay with a 50 DM note. What's the smallest number of coins and notes you can get as change? (see p.28)

CASHING A TRAVELLER'S CHEQUE

8   You're running short of money. So into the bank to cash a traveller's cheque (*einen Reisescheck*) for 400 DM.

ANGESTELLTER	Guten Tag.
SIE	_____ .
ANGESTELLTER	Ja, gerne. Unterschreiben Sie bitte hier.
SIE	(Here?)
ANGESTELLTER	Ja bitte . . . So, das macht dann dreihundert-sechsundneunzig Mark fünfzig. Bitte sehr.
SIE	_____ .

9   How many marks did he give you?
10   How much commission did he charge?

WORTH KNOWING

SHOPPING HOURS

From Monday to Friday shops in Germany are usually open from 9 a.m. to 6.30 p.m. Some food shops or kiosks may be open earlier, while small shops might be closed for one or two hours during lunchtime. On Thursdays most shops in city centres are open until 8.30 p.m. On Saturdays shops close at noon or 2 p.m., but the first Saturday of the month is *langer Samstag (lit.* 'long Saturday'), which means they stay open in summer until 4.30 and in winter until 6 p.m.

POSTING YOUR LETTERS AND POSTCARDS

Stamps are available at post offices (or sometimes from small stationers' or souvenir shops). Ordinary letters and postcards to other EC countries cost the same as post within Germany. But postcards cost less than letters!

Postboxes are yellow and in towns and cities are emptied several times a day. Telephone boxes are also yellow, although there are plans to change them to white in the near future.

Post offices are generally open between   and 12 a.m. and 3 and   p.m.

AT THE BAKER'S

There's an enormous variety of bread and rolls in German bakers' shops. There are about twenty different kinds of rolls, ranging from soft rolls, poppy seed rolls (*Mohnbrötchen*) and rye rolls (*Roggenbrötchen*) to rolls with onions (*Zwiebeln*) or sunflower seeds (*Sonnenblumensamen*) inside. Often they're baked from the full grain (*Vollkornbrötchen*) or from more than one kind of grain (*Mehrkornbrötchen*). There are about the same number of bread varieties, which are all worth a try. Bread varies from white (*Weißbrot*) to very dark (*Schwarzbrot*). It comes in all shapes and sizes, and in many different flavours. Try *Kümmelbrot* (with caraway seeds), *Zwiebelbrot* (with onions) or *Sonnenblumenbrot* (with sunflower seeds), for example.

GERMAN WINE

As with bread, the choice of wines is enormous and you'll never manage to taste them all. Most wines come from the Rhine or Moselle regions. German wines are mostly white; only in a very few areas, such as the Ahr, is red wine grown.

Herr Pluschke offered Frau Harrington a 'Marienburger Riesling' from the Moselle region. Riesling is a traditional grape, called 'The Queen of Grapes', *Königin der Trauben*.

CHANGING MONEY

You can change cash, traveller's cheques or eurocheques at most banks and post offices. Additionally there are a growing number of cash machines that accept foreign cash cards or credit cards.

In shops the use of credit cards is not as widespread as in the UK or USA. Smaller shops often don't accept them and even in department stores you may be sent to a different cashpoint if you want to pay with 'plastic'. You can't buy train tickets with credit cards, but they're useful for car hire, eating out or paying your hotel bill.

3 FINDING SOMEWHERE TO STAY

KEY WORDS AND PHRASES

BOOKING A HOTEL ROOM

ich möchte ein Zimmer reservieren	I'd like to book a room
ein Doppelzimmer oder ein Einzelzimmer?	a double room or a single room?
mit Dusche oder mit Bad?	with shower or with bath?

FOR HOW LONG?

für . . .	for . . .
eine Nacht	one night
zwei Nächte	two nights
eine Woche	a week
drei Tage	three days

AT THE CAMP SITE

haben Sie noch (Zelt) Plätze frei?	have you still got any (tent) pitches available?
wir haben . . .	we've got . . .
ein Zelt	a tent
einen Wohnwagen	a caravan

CONVERSATIONS

AT THE TOURIST INFORMATION CENTRE

I'd like to book a double room. With shower.

HERR HINZE	Ich möchte ein Zimmer reservieren.
FRAU HERBST	Ja, gern. Möchten Sie ein Doppelzimmer oder ein Einzelzimmer?
HERR HINZE	Ein Doppelzimmer.
FRAU HERBST	Mit Dusche oder mit Bad?
HERR HINZE	Mit Dusche.
FRAU HERBST	Ja, und für wie viele Nächte möchten Sie bleiben?
HERR HINZE	Für zwei Nächte.

A single room. If possible with bath. For a week.

FRAU PAGITZ	Ich möchte gerne ein Zimmer reservieren.
FRAU HERBST	Was für ein Zimmer möchten Sie reservieren, ein Einzelzimmer oder ein Doppelzimmer?
FRAU PAGITZ	Ein Einzelzimmer.
FRAU HERBST	Ein Einzelzimmer mit Dusche oder mit Bad?
FRAU PAGITZ	Wenn es geht, mit Bad.
FRAU HERBST	Und für wie viele Nächte möchten Sie bleiben?
FRAU PAGITZ	Für eine Woche.
FRAU HERBST	Und wie ist, bitte, Ihr Name?
FRAU PAGITZ	Pagitz.
FRAU HERBST	Gut, Frau Pagitz, ich kann Ihnen ein Zimmer anbieten im Hotel am Dammtor.
FRAU PAGITZ	Und was kostet es?
FRAU HERBST	Das Zimmer kostet neunzig Mark.
FRAU PAGITZ	Ja, das geht.

AT THE HOTEL

Have you got a room? A single with bath, please.

FRAU DEBUS	Haben Sie ein Zimmer frei?
EMPFANG	Was hätten Sie denn gerne? Ein Einzelzimmer oder ein Doppelzimmer?
FRAU DEBUS	Ein Einzelzimmer mit Bad, bitte . . .

I've booked a room. For two nights.

HERR BESSEN	Mein Name ist Bessen. Ich habe ein Zimmer reserviert.
FRAU STORM	Ja. Herzlich willkommen, Herr Bessen.
HERR BESSEN	Danke schön.
FRAU STORM	Das war ein Einzelzimmer für zwei Nächte.
HERR BESSEN	Ja.
FRAU STORM	Wenn ich Sie gerade noch bitten darf, sich hier einzutragen.
HERR BESSEN	Ja.
FRAU STORM	Adresse . . .
HERR BESSEN	Ja.
FRAU STORM	Und Unterschrift.

This is your key. Room 75 on the first floor.

FRAU KRÜGER	Dürfte ich Sie bitten, sich einzutragen?
HERR KOTHE	Ja, sicher.
FRAU KRÜGER	Danke.
HERR KOTHE	*(handing back the form)* Bitte sehr.
FRAU KRÜGER	Danke sehr. Das ist Ihr Zimmerschlüssel. Zimmer fünfundsiebzig in der ersten Etage.

This is room 75. I'd like breakfast in my room, please.

FRAU KRÜGER	*(answering the phone)* Empfang, guten Morgen.
HERR KOTHE	Guten Morgen. Hier ist Zimmer fünfundsiebzig. Ich hätte gern ein Frühstück aufs Zimmer.

FRAU KRÜGER	Mit Kaffee oder Tee?
HERR KOTHE	Kaffee, bitte.
FRAU KRÜGER	Haben Sie sonst noch irgendwelche extra Wünsche?
HERR KOTHE	Nein, danke.
FRAU KRÜGER	Bitte sehr. Das Frühstück kommt dann sofort.
HERR KOTHE	Vielen Dank. Auf Wiederhören.
FRAU KRÜGER	Wiederhören.

Can you order me a taxi, please? Room 75.

HERR KOTHE	Können Sie mir bitte ein Taxi bestellen?
FRAU KRÜGER	Aber sehr gerne. Wie ist, bitte, Ihre Zimmernummer?
HERR KOTHE	Fünfundsiebzig.
FRAU KRÜGER	*(ringing for a taxi)* Guten Morgen, Hotel Bellevue. Ich bräuchte eine Taxe auf Zimmer fünfundsiebzig. Danke. *(to Herr Kothe)* Die Taxe kommt sofort.

May I have my key, please?

HERR BESSEN	Darf ich meinen Schlüssel bitte haben?
FRAU STORM	Ja. Und welche Zimmernummer?
HERR BESSEN	Dreihunderteinundzwanzig.
FRAU STORM	Ja. *(handing him the key)* So, bitte schön, Herr Bessen.
HERR BESSEN	Danke schön.

I'd like the bill, please. I'm paying by credit card.

HERR KOTHE	Ich hätte gern die Rechnung.
FRAU KRÜGER	Wie ist bitte Ihre Zimmernummer?
HERR KOTHE	Fünfundsiebzig.
FRAU KRÜGER	Danke. Kommt etwas aus der Minibar dazu?
HERR KOTHE	Ja. Ich hatte einen Whisky.
FRAU KRÜGER	Danke schön. Und wie möchten Sie bezahlen?

HERR KOTHE	Mit Kreditkarte, bitte.
FRAU KRÜGER	Ja, danke. *(takes the imprint)* Dürfte ich Sie bitten, zu unterschreiben?

AT THE CAMP SITE

I'm here with a caravan. Have you still got spaces available?

HR. LÜDERMANN	Schön' guten Tag, kann ich Ihnen helfen?
HERR HINZE	Ja. Ich bin hier mit einem Wohnwagen. Haben Sie noch Plätze frei?
HR. LÜDERMANN	Ja. Wir haben noch Plätze zur Verfügung.
HERR HINZE	Wir möchten gerne drei Tage bleiben, ist das möglich?
HR. LÜDERMANN	Das wäre möglich, ja.
HERR HINZE	Und was kostet das?
HR. LÜDERMANN	Wie viele Personen sind Sie?
HERR HINZE	Wir sind zwei Erwachsene und zwei Kinder.
HR. LÜDERMANN	Pro Erwachsener bezahlen Sie vier Mark, pro Kind drei Mark, für den Wohnwagen zwölf Mark fünfzig und für den PKW vier Mark.

Have you still got tent pitches available? We have two bikes.

FRAU PAGITZ	Haben Sie noch Zeltplätze frei?
HR. LÜDERMANN	Wir haben noch Zeltplätze zur Verfügung. Wie groß ist denn Ihr Zelt?
FRAU PAGITZ	Es ist ein Zweipersonenzelt.
HR. LÜDERMANN	Sind Sie zwei Personen?
FRAU PAGITZ	Ja.
HR. LÜDERMANN	Haben Sie ein Fahrzeug dabei?
FRAU PAGITZ	Ja, wir haben zwei Fahrräder.

WORD LIST

bleiben	to stay
was für . . . ?	what kind of . . . ?
Ihr Name	your name
ich kann . . . anbieten	I can offer . . .
das geht	that's OK
was hätten sie denn gern?	what (kind of room) would you like?
herzlich willkommen!	you're very welcome!
wenn ich Sie gerade noch bitten darf . . .	if I can just ask you . . .
sich hier einzutragen	to register here
die Adresse	address
die Unterschrift	signature
dürfte ich Sie bitten . . . ?	could I ask you . . . ?
sicher	certainly
der Empfang	reception
sonst noch irgendwelche extra Wünsche	any other extra requests
sofort	straight away
(auf) Wiederhören	goodbye (on the phone)
Ihre Zimmernummer	your room number
ich bräuchte . . .	I need, please . . .
etwas aus der Minibar	anything from the minibar
ich hatte . . .	I had . . .
bezahlen	to pay
unterschreiben	to sign
der Campingplatz	camp site
zur Verfügung	available
das wäre möglich	that would be possible
wie viele Personen?	how many people?
zwei Erwachsene	two adults
zwei Kinder	two children
pro . . .	per . . .

der PKW (Personenkraftwagen)	car
das Zelt	tent
das Fahrzeug	vehicle
zwei Fahrräder	two bicycles
der Platzwart	campsite warden

EXPLANATIONS

CHECKING IN

Are rooms/spaces available?
haben Sie Zimmer/(Zelt)Plätze frei?
If you've booked a room in advance:
ich habe ein Zimmer reserviert
If you want a room on the spot or for a future date:
ich möchte ein Zimmer reservieren

What sort of room?
ein Einzelzimmer oder ein Doppelzimmer
mit Bad oder mit Dusche
mit zwei Betten (though rooms with twin beds are not often available in German hotels!)

At the camp site:

wir haben | *ein Zelt*
 | *einen Wohnwagen*

wir sind | *zwei Erwachsene*
 | *zwei Erwachsene und zwei Kinder*

How long do you want to stay?

für | *eine Nacht, zwei Nächte*
 | *eine Woche, zwei Wochen*

And how much is it?
was kostet es? or *wieviel kostet es?*

WIEVIEL? WIE VIELE?

wieviel? (how much?) is written as one word, *wie viele?* (how many?) as two:
wieviel kostet es?
wie viele Personen sind Sie?
But in spoken German people often say *wieviel?* for both 'how much?' and 'how many?'

MY/YOUR

Instead of *der/die/das* (the) or *ein/eine/ein* (a) you may want to use the possessive *mein* (m.)/*meine* (f.)/*mein* (n.), meaning 'my', or *Ihr* (m.)/*Ihre* (f.)/*Ihr* (n.), meaning 'your'.

wie ist | *Ihr Name* (m.)?
| *Ihre Zimmernummer* (f.)?
wie groß ist *Ihr Zelt* (n.)?

mein Name (m.) *ist Bessen*
meine Zimmernummer (f.) *ist 75*
mein Zelt (n.) *ist ein Zweipersonenzelt*

You may have noticed other endings on words like *ein, mein, Ihr:*
darf ich meinen Schlüssel bitte haben?
ich bin hier mit meinem Wohnwagen
After most verbs you use *den, meinen, Ihren,* etc. with masculine nouns (i.e. when they're the direct object).

But don't worry if you get the endings wrong. You'll still be understood.

PLURALS

In English you say 'one room' but 'two rooms', 'one child' but 'two children', 'one loaf' but 'two loaves', 'one sheep' or 'two sheep', and so on. There are a number of different ways of forming plurals in German, too. The noun may add an ending or an *Umlaut* or both. Or it may not change at all. The best way of getting plurals right is to learn them as you go along. In the word list at the end of the book what you add to make a noun plural is given in brackets, like this:

SINGULAR	PLURAL
die Woche (-n)	*die Wochen*
das Hotel (-s)	*die Hotels*
der Tag (-e)	*die Tage*
die Nacht (-̈e)	*die Nächte*
das Kind (-er)	*die Kinder*
das Zimmer (-)	*die Zimmer*

With all plural nouns the word for 'the' is *die,* 'my' is *meine* and 'your' is *Ihre*.

BITTE SCHÖN

In German you'll hear *bitte* or *bitte schön* or *bitte sehr* all the time. You say it if someone thanks you, in the sense of 'not at all'. You also say it when you're handing someone something or doing them some kind of service, opening the door perhaps, or passing them something at the table. Then it means something like 'there you are'.

AUF WIEDERHÖREN!

On the phone you don't say *auf Wiedersehen* (*lit.* until we see each other again) but *auf Wiederhören* (until we hear each other again). But that may change with the introduction of picture-phones!

TELEPHONING A HOTEL

1   At the station you see a free hotel telephone. You decide to try to get a room at the Hotel zur Post.

EMPFANG	*(answering the phone)* Hotel zur Post, guten Tag. Bitte schön?
SIE	(Say good day, and tell her you'd like a single room with a shower.)
EMPFANG	Ja, sicherlich, das haben wir.
SIE	(Inquire about the price.)
EMPFANG	Das kostet hundertfünf Mark pro Nacht.
SIE	(Oh! Don't accept.)
EMPFANG	Schade! Tut mir leid. Auf Wiederhören.

AT THE TOURIST INFORMATION CENTRE

2   After that you decide to go to the tourist information centre and ask for a room there. What do you say?

ANGESTELLTE	Guten Tag. Was kann ich für Sie tun?
SIE	(You'd like to book a room.)
ANGESTELLTE	Ja, gern. Was für ein Zimmer möchten Sie?
SIE	(A single room with a shower.)
ANGESTELLTE	Und für wie viele Nächte möchten Sie bleiben?
SIE	(Four nights, please.)
ANGESTELLTE	Ich kann Ihnen ein sehr schönes Zimmer im Palast Hotel anbieten.
SIE	(Inquire about the price.)
ANGESTELLTE	Das Zimmer kostet achtzig Mark pro Nacht.
SIE	(Accept.)

CHECKING IN

3 You arrive at the Palast Hotel and check in. As you're in a hurry to get to an appointment you ask for a taxi straightaway.

EMPFANG	Guten Tag. Bitte sehr?
SIE	(Introduce yourself, and say you've booked a room.)
EMPFANG	Ja, richtig. Ein Einzelzimmer für vier Nächte. Möchten Sie ein Zimmer mit Bad oder mit Dusche?
SIE	(With a shower.)
EMPFANG	Gut. Dürfte ich Sie bitten, sich einzutragen?
SIE	(Hand back the form.)
EMPFANG	Danke sehr. Hier ist Ihr Schlüssel. Zimmer hundertsiebzehn in der ersten Etage. Kann ich sonst noch etwas für Sie tun?
SIE	(Ask if she can order you a taxi.)
EMPFANG	Ja, sicher. *(phones for a taxi)* Es kommt gleich.
SIE	(Thank her.)

ROOM SERVICE

4 Back in your room you'd like a drink. You call reception.

EMPFANG	*(answering the phone)* Empfang. Bitte sehr?
SIE	(You'd like a bottle of wine.)
EMPFANG	Gern. Roten oder weißen?
SIE	(White, please.)
EMPFANG	Darf es sonst noch etwas sein?
SIE	(Yes, a bottle of mineral water, please.)
EMPFANG	Vielen Dank. Kommt sofort. Wiederhören.
SIE	(Thank you and goodbye.)

AT THE CAMP SITE

5 Travelling by car and with a tent you've arrived at a camp site. What do you say to the attendant?

PLATZWART	Guten Tag, die Herrschaften. Was kann ich für Sie tun?
SIE	(Ask if he's still got tent pitches available.)
PLATZWART	Ja, sicherlich. Wie viele Personen sind Sie?
SIE	(You're three adults and a child.)
PLATZWART	Haben Sie ein Fahrzeug?
SIE	(Answer and ask the price.)
PLATZWART	Die Erwachsenen kosten sechs Mark, das Kind kostet vier Mark, und das Auto kostet dreizehn Mark fünfzig pro Nacht.
SIE	(Accept.)

WORTH KNOWING

HOTELS

In Germany there are no official hotel categories, but hotels often give themselves unofficial ratings ranging from one to five stars, and 'luxury' for the very best.

Hamburg's most famous hotel is the *Vier Jahreszeiten*, listed among the world's ten leading Grand Hotels. Situated directly on the *Binnenalster*, it's ideal for an after-shopping tea or a meal in one of its two superb restaurants.

TOURIST INFORMATION

A tourist information centre can be found in almost every town, often in or near the town hall. It's often called *der Verkehrsverein* or *der Fremdenverkehrsverein* but you can usually recognise it by the international sign 'i' (for *Information*). You can book accommodation via the tourist information centre although – especially when you're on holiday and have the time – you might be better advised to have a look round the hotels yourself first, to find the place that suits you best.

Tourist information centres can give you plenty of advice about what to see and do and they often sell theatre or concert tickets as well.

REGISTRATION

By law everybody booking into any kind of public accommodation is required to register. Information about guests (name, home address, signature) is routinely given to the police.

CAMPING

You can find camp sites for caravans or tents all over Germany. Standards and prices vary considerably and it's a good idea to enquire before travelling. Advance bookings are often necessary, especially during the holiday season. For further information contact the ADAC (*Allgemeiner Deutscher Automobil-Club,* the German automobile association) near your destination or as soon as you enter the country.

4 GETTING ABOUT

KEY WORDS AND PHRASES

FINDING OUT WHERE PLACES ARE

wo ist . . . ?	where is . . . ?
(wo) gibt es . . . ?	(where) is there . . . ?
hier in der Nähe?	near here?

. . . AND HOW TO GET THERE

wie komme ich . . .	how do I get . . .
zum Jungfernstieg?	to the Jungfernstieg?
zur Autobahn?	to the motorway?
nach Bremen?	to Bremen?

SOME KEY DIRECTIONS

Sie gehen	you go
Sie fahren	you drive
rechts	on/to the right
links	on/to the left
geradeaus	straight ahead
um die Ecke	round the corner
über (die Brücke)	across (the bridge)
die nächste/erste/zweite Straße	the next/first/second street
auf der rechten/linken Seite	on the right-hand/left-hand side

<table>
<tbody>
<tr><td colspan="2">TRAVELLING BY TRAIN</td></tr>
<tr><td>einmal/zweimal</td><td>one/two tickets (once/twice)</td></tr>
<tr><td>erster zweiter Klasse</td><td>first/second class</td></tr>
<tr><td>einfache Fahrt</td><td>single</td></tr>
<tr><td>hin und zurück</td><td>return</td></tr>
</tbody>
</table>

CONVERSATIONS

ASKING DIRECTIONS

Excuse me, where's the nearest bus-stop?

FR. HARRINGTON   Entschuldigen Sie bitte, wo ist die nächste Bushaltestelle?

FRAU RADTKE   Die nächste Bushaltestelle ist gleich hier nebenan, um die nächste Ecke. Da fährt der Bus ab.

Where's the art gallery, please? Is it far?

FRAU PAGITZ   Wo ist die Kunsthalle, bitte?

FRAU HERBST   Sie gehen bitte die nächste Straße rechts hinunter, links über die Brücke, und dann sehen Sie direkt das Gebäude.

FRAU PAGITZ   Ist das weit?

FRAU HERBST   Das ist ungefähr zwei Minuten zu Fuß.

FRAU PAGITZ   Ah, wunderbar. Danke schön.

Is there a pharmacy nearby? I'm a stranger here.

HERR HINZE   Entschuldigen Sie bitte, gibt es hier in der Nähe eine Apotheke?

FRAU HERBST   Ja, natürlich. Die Hauptbahnhofapotheke. Die ist direkt über den Hachmannplatz hinüber auf der rechten Seite.

HERR HINZE   Und wo ist der Hachmannplatz? Ich bin fremd hier.

FRAU HERBST	Direkt hier vor dem Haus.
HERR HINZE	Ah, danke schön.
FRAU HERBST	Bitte.

Where's there a supermarket near here?

FRAU HADRIAN	Wo gibt es hier einen Supermarkt?
BEAMTER	Wenn Sie diese Straße entlang gehen etwa fünf Minuten, dann finden Sie ihn auf der rechten Seite.
FRAU HADRIAN	Danke schön.

What's the best way to the Jungfernstieg? I'd like to walk.

HERR KOTHE	Entschuldigen Sie bitte, wie komme ich am besten zum Jungfernstieg?
FRAU KRÜGER	Möchten Sie zu Fuß gehen?
HERR KOTHE	Ja, ich möchte zu Fuß gehen.
FRAU KRÜGER	Da gehen Sie einfach hier links, geradeaus immer an der Alster lang. Da kommen Sie automatisch zum Jungfernstieg.
HERR KOTHE	Und wie weit ist das?
FRAU KRÜGER	Zu Fuß zirka fünfzehn Minuten.

How do I get to the Bremen motorway? Ah, it's signposted.

FR. HARRINGTON	Wie komme ich zur Autobahn nach Bremen?
HERR HINZE	Oh, da muß ich einen Moment überlegen. Sie fahren hier weiter geradeaus, dann die zweite links. Und dann ist es die erste wieder rechts. Und da ist ein Schild 'Autobahn Bremen'.
FR. HARRINGTON	Ach, es ist ausgeschildert.
HERR HINZE	Ja.
FR. HARRINGTON	Das ist ja gut.

What's the quickest way to the Ost-West-Straße? *Is it very far from here?*

DR. GÖTTSCH　　Wie komme ich denn am schnellsten zur Ost-West-Straße?

FRAU PETERS　　Das ist ganz einfach von hier. Sie sind jetzt beim alten Elbtunnel, da fahren Sie geradeaus bis zur nächsten Ampel und biegen nach links in die Helgoländer Allee ein. Da fahren Sie bis zum Millerntorplatz weiter und dann rechts in die Ost-West-Straße.

DR. GÖTTSCH　　Ist es sehr weit von hier?

FRAU PETERS　　Ach, nur ein paar Minuten.

AROUND THE CITY

At the hairdresser's. *What are your opening hours?*

FR. HARRINGTON　Wie sind Ihre Öffnungszeiten?

FRAU RADTKE　　Wir haben von Montag bis Freitag von acht Uhr dreißig bis achtzehn Uhr geöffnet, und sonnabends von acht bis zwölf Uhr.

At the Tourist Information Centre. *I'd like to go on a city tour. When does the next one leave?*

HERR HINZE　　Ich möchte gerne eine Stadtrundfahrt machen. Wann geht denn die nächste?

FRAU HERBST　　Die nächste Stadtrundfahrt ist um vierzehn Uhr.

HERR HINZE　　Und was kostet die?

FRAU HERBST　　Pro Person zweiundzwanzig Mark.

HERR HINZE　　Ja, dann hätte ich gern zwei Karten.

Booking a trip round Hamburg harbour. *Two adults, please. How long does the trip last?*

HR. BRINKMANN　Hafenrundfahrt hier! Hier die Abfahrt! Wollen Sie auch noch mit? Hier gleich eine

Abfahrt! Einsteigen, mitreisen! Hafenrundfahrt hier!

FRAU EVRAHR	Guten Tag. Zwei Erwachsene, bitte.
HR. BRINKMANN	Zwei Erwachsene, à Person zwölf Mark, vierundzwanzig Mark, bitte.
FRAU EVRAHR	Wie lange dauert die Fahrt?
HR. BRINKMANN	Eine gute Stunde.

BUS AND TRAIN

What number (bus) goes to the city centre?

FR. HARRINGTON	Welche Nummer fährt in die Innenstadt?
FRAU RADTKE	Der Hundertsiebenundfünziger.
FR. HARRINGTON	Vielen Dank.

At the station. One second-class ticket to Würzburg, please. Return.

HERR KOTHE	Einmal zweiter Klasse nach Würzburg, bitte.
BEAMTER	Einfache Fahrt oder hin und zurück?
HERR KOTHE	Hin und zurück, bitte.
BEAMTER	Einen Moment, bitte.

WORD LIST

gleich hier nebenan	just near here
fährt ab	leaves
die nächste Straße hinunter	down the next street
sehen	to see
direkt	direct(ly), right in front of you
das Gebäude	building
ist das weit?	is that far?
ungefähr zwei Minuten	about two minutes
zu Fuß	on foot
wunderbar	wonderful
natürlich	of course

der Hauptbahnhof	main station
vor	in front of
wenn	if
diese Straße entlang	along this street
etwa = ungefähr	about
finden	to find
der Jungfernstieg	street in Hamburg (*lit.* 'path of the virgins')
einfach	simple, simply
dann kommen Sie zu . . .	then you'll come to . . .
automatisch	automatically
zirka = ungefähr	about
ich muß überlegen	I must think
das Schild	sign
das ist ganz einfach	that's quite simple
bis zur (nächsten Ampel)	up to the (next traffic light)
einbiegen in	to turn into
weiter	(further) on
geöffnet	open
geschlossen	closed
von . . . bis	from . . . to (until)
die (Fahr)karte	ticket
die Abfahrt	departure
wollen Sie auch noch mit?	do you want to come as well?
einsteigen	to board
eine gute Stunde	a good hour

EXPLANATIONS

ASKING WHERE PLACES ARE

wo ist | *der Bahnhof* (m.)?
die Kunsthalle (f.)?
das Hotel Bellevue (n.)?

(wo) gibt es hier | *einen Supermarkt* (m.)?
 | *eine Apotheke* (f.)?
 | *ein Postamt* (n.)? *(post office)*

With a masculine noun, after *gibt es* you use *einen*.

FINDING OUT HOW TO GET THERE

wie komme ich . . .

am besten | *zum Jungfernstieg* (m.) ?
am schnellsten | *zur Autobahn* (f.) ?
 | *zum Hotel Bellevue* (n.) ?
 | *nach Bremen?*

Notice that with a masculine or neuter noun you use *zum (= zu dem)*, with a feminine noun *zur (=zu der)* and with names of towns (and most countries) *nach*.

GEHEN OR *FAHREN*?

Gehen and *fahren* both mean 'to go'. You use *gehen* when walking is involved, but to travel by any means of transport is *fahren*. So it's:

mit dem Bus
mit dem Taxi
mit dem Zug (train) | *fahren*
mit dem Auto
mit dem Fahrrad
mit der Straßenbahn

But: *zu Fuß gehen*

FIRST, SECOND, THIRD, ETC.

Numbers between 1 and 19 mostly add '. . . *te*':
zwei   *der zweite* (second)

fünf   *der fünfte* (fifth)
zehn   *der zehnte* (tenth)
dreizehn   *der dreizehnte* (thirteenth)
But note these:
eins   *der erste* (first)
drei   *der dritte* (third)

Numbers from 20 onwards add '. . . *ste*':
zweiundzwanzig – der zweiundzwanzigste (twenty-second)
neunundvierzig –   *der neunundvierzigste* (forty-ninth)

Written as figures (for example in dates) these endings are
indicated by a full stop:
22. April – der zweiundzwanzigste April
3. September – der dritte September

DAYS OF THE WEEK

SEPTEMBER	WOCHE 39
MONTAG 23 *THEATER (LOHENGRIN)*	
DIENSTAG 24 *DR. MÜLLER (ZAHNARZT)* *HAUPTBAHNHOF (PETER ABHOLEN)*	
MITTWOCH 25 *ALSTERPAVILLON MIT SUSANNE*	
DONNERSTAG 26 *FRISEUR !* *SKAT IN DER "GLOCKE"*	
FREITAG 27 *MITTAGESSEN IM HOTEL* *BELLEVUE MIT BARBARA*	
SAMSTAG 28 *MARKT !*	
SONNTAG 29 *OMA*	

Particularly in North Germany, people often say *Sonnabend*
instead of *Samstag*.

TIME

To find out the time, ask: *wieviel Uhr ist es?* To tell someone the time, start with: *es ist . . .* 'Past' is *nach* and 'to' is *vor*:

Es ist
| *neun Uhr* (9 o'clock)
| *fünf nach neun* (five past . . .)
| *Viertel nach neun* (quarter past . . .)
| *Viertel vor zehn* (quarter to . . .)
| *zehn vor zehn* (ten to . . .)

But be careful with 'half past'! Germans think of the hour ahead. 'Half past six' is 'half way to seven', *halb sieben*. 'Half past ten' is 'half way to eleven', *halb elf.*

In official situations, and often in ordinary conversation as well, people use the 24–hour clock:
es ist sechzehn Uhr zwanzig
es ist zweiundzwanzig Uhr fünfundvierzig

'At' a time is *um*:
die nächste Stadtrundfahrt ist um vierzehn Uhr

And 'from . . . to . . .' is *von . . . bis . . . :*
wir haben von acht Uhr dreißig bis achtzehn Uhr geöffnet

BUYING TRAIN TICKETS

You need to say:
how many tickets: *einmal, zweimal, . . .*
first or second class: *erster oder zweiter Klasse*
single or return: *einfach oder hin und zurück*
where you're going: *nach Bremen*

EXERCISES

GOING BY UNDERGROUND

1 It's your first morning in Hamburg and you want to explore the city. At the hotel reception you ask where the nearest underground station is:

SIE   _____ ?

EMPFANG   Die nächste U-Bahn Station ist zwei Straßen weiter, gleich links um die Ecke.

2 At the underground station you inquire which number goes to the city centre.

SIE   _____ ?

MANN   Die U 3 fährt in die Innenstadt.

FINDING A CAFÉ

3 After some sightseeing you feel like a coffee. You stop a passer-by and ask if there's a café nearby.

SIE   _____ ?

PASSANT   Ja, sicher. Sie gehen über die Alsterallee, biegen links in die erste Straße und gehen immer geradeaus. Dann die zweite Straße rechts gehen Sie bis zur Hamburger Straße. Direkt links an der Ecke ist ein schönes Café.

SIE   (Inquire if it's far.)

PASSANT   Nein. Nur ungefähr zehn Minuten zu Fuß.

4 As you've got a town map *(overleaf)* you mark in the position of the café:

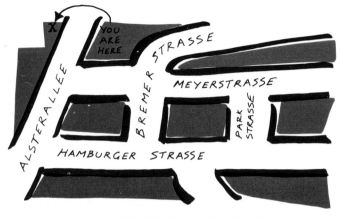

WHEN IS THE BANK OPEN?

5 On the way to the café you pass a bank. You go in to inquire about opening hours.

SIE   _____ ?

ANGESTELLTER   Wir haben von Montag bis Mittwoch von neun bis sechzehn Uhr dreißig geöffnet, am Donnerstag von neun bis achtzehn Uhr und am Freitag von neun bis vierzehn Uhr dreißig.

SIE   (Ask if they're open on Saturdays.)

ANGESTELLTER   Sonnabends haben wir nicht geöffnet.

6 Did you understand the times? See if you can complete the notice:

DEUTSCHE BANK, HAMBURG		
ÖFFNUNGSZEITEN:		
Mo./Di./Mi.:	_____ Uhr bis	_____ Uhr
Donnerstag:	_____ Uhr bis	_____ Uhr
Freitag:	_____ Uhr bis	_____ Uhr
Samstag:		

WHICH SIGHTSEEING TRIP?

7 Seeing the tourist information centre you decide to go on a sightseeing tour. You enjoy boat trips, it's Tuesday and about 2 p.m., you have to be back at your hotel by 5.30 p.m. and it takes you about 45 minutes to get there. Which of these trips do you choose?

HAMBURG SEHEN UND LIEBEN!

Unsere Rundfahrten geben Ihnen den besten Eindruck:

Große Stadtrundfahrt mit Hafenrundfahrt
täglich 10 und 14 Uhr
Dauer etwa 3 Stunden

Große Stadtrundfahrt
täglich 11, 13 und 15 Uhr
Dauer ca. 2 Stunden

Große Hafenrundfahrt
Mittwoch, Sonnabend und Sonntag jeweils 11 und 15 Uhr
Dauer ca. 1¼ Stunde

Kleine Stadtrundfahrt mit Alster-Bootsfahrt
täglich 10.30, 14.30 und 16 Uhr
Dauer ca. 2 Stunden

Kombinierte Hafenrundfahrt und Alsterfahrt
Dienstag, Donnerstag, Samstag 12 und 15 Uhr
Dauer ca. 2½ Stunden

WORTH KNOWING

PUBLIC TRANSPORT

Bus- and tram-stops in Germany are signed by a green H (for *Haltestelle*) in a green circle on a yellow background. Underground systems are indicated by the familiar U (for *Untergrundbahn*) and the fast local railway system by S (for *Schnellbahn*). Often you can use the same ticket on all of them, but it's wise to check if you don't want to be caught with an invalid ticket by the ticket inspector.

Queuing (unfortunately) isn't a German habit, and everybody just pushes forward as soon as the vehicle arrives.

You can buy bus and tram tickets in advance from slot machines or tobacconists. If you don't have a ticket, get in the front car as they are only available from the driver. For the underground or *S-Bahn* you also have to get a ticket in advance, usually from a slot machine at the station.

BUYING MEDICINES

In Germany only pharmacies *(Apotheken)* sell drugs, though a few, mainly 'natural', medicines may be bought at chemists' *(Drogerien)* or in supermarkets.

There are always a number of pharmacies open at night for emergencies. You'll find a list on display at any pharmacy in town.

GERMAN RAILWAYS

The *Deutsche Bundesbahn* – still the *Deutsche Reichsbahn* in eastern parts – provides an excellent service throughout the country. Rapid *InterCity (IC)* trains connect all important cities every hour, while *EuroCity (EC)* trains run direct into neighbouring countries. To get you there even sooner, new tracks are currently under construction for these fast services and for *InterCity Expreß (ICE)* trains. When travelling InterCity or EuroCity you have to pay a supplement (*der Zuschlag*).

FD-Züge or *Fernschnellzüge* (long–distance expresses) and *D-Züge* or *Schnellzüge* (ordinary expresses) also link major cities (a supplement is usually required for journeys under 50 km). More local services are provided by Inter–Regio, *E-Züge* or *Eilzüge* (fast stopping trains) and *Personenzüge* (slow stopping trains).

MORE ABOUT TIME

Germans sometimes count minutes to or past the half hour (often between twenty minutes past and twenty minutes to the hour):

25 past 3   *fünf vor halb vier*
                         (five minutes to half past three)
27 minutes to 8 *drei nach halb acht*
                         (three minutes past half past seven)

You needn't use this way of saying the time yourself, but understanding it could be useful.

5 EATING OUT

ORDERING

die Speisekarte, bitte	the menu, please
die Scholle, bitte	the plaice, please
ich nehme . . .	I'll have . . .
für mich . . .	for me . . .
das Zitronensorbet	the lemon sorbet
einen trockenen Sherry	a dry sherry

THE WAITER MAY ASK:

haben Sie schon gewählt?	have you chosen?
hat es Ihnen geschmeckt?	did you enjoy it?
darf ich Ihnen noch etwas anbieten?	may I offer you anything else?
guten Appetit!	enjoy your meal!

CONVERSATIONS

BREAKFAST, COFFEE, TEA, CAKES

Breakfast at the Hotel Bellevue. Coffee, please.

OBER   Guten Morgen, der Herr. Möchten Sie Kaffee, Tee . . . ?

HERR KOTHE	Kaffee, bitte.
OBER	Ja, bring' ich Ihnen sofort. Wir haben ein Frühstücksbüffet, möchten Sie sich daran bedienen?
HERR KOTHE	Ja, gern.

At the Alsterpavillon. *Two pots of coffee. And a piece of apple strudel, please. With cream.*

OBER	Ja, bitte?
FRAU EVRAHR	Bitte zwei Kännchen Kaffee, und für mich ein Stück Nußtorte.
OBER	*(to Herr Knuth)* Und für Sie, bitte?
HERR KNUTH	Ein Stück Apfelstrudel, bitte.
OBER	Den Apfelstrudel mit Sahne oder ohne Sahne?
HERR KNUTH	Mit Sahne.

At a café. *A glass of tea. May I have your 'cake ticket', please?*

KELLNERIN	Guten Tag. Bitte schön?
KUNDIN	Ich hätte gerne ein Glas Tee.
KELLNERIN	Ja, gerne. Bekommen Sie auch Kuchen?
KUNDIN	Ja, ich hab' ein Stück Himbeertorte bestellt.
KELLNERIN	Dann geben Sie mir bitte Ihren Kuchenbon.
KUNDIN	Bitte schön.

DINNER AT THE HOTEL

Here's the menu. *Would you like an aperitif first?*

OBER	Guten Tag, der Herr. Möchten Sie speisen?
HERR KOTHE	Ja, bitte.
OBER	Hier, die Speisekarte für Sie.
HERR KOTHE	Vielen Dank.
OBER	Möchten Sie vorab einen Aperitif trinken?
HERR KOTHE	Ja . . . ich nehme einen trockenen Sherry, bitte.

As a starter I'd like the Hamburg crayfish soup. Then the
plaice, please. And a Franconian wine, a nice dry one.

OBER	Der Herr, haben Sie schon gewählt?
HERR KOTHE	Ja, als Vorspeise hätte ich gern die Hamburger Krebssuppe.
OBER	Und als Hauptgang?
HERR KOTHE	Die Scholle, bitte.
OBER	Ja. Und Sie trinken dazu?
HERR KOTHE	Einen Frankenwein, glaub' ich.
OBER	Einen schönen trockenen Frankenwein?
HERR KOTHE	Ja, bitte.

It was excellent. I'll have the lemon sorbet, please.

OBER	So, der Herr, hat's Ihnen geschmeckt?
HERR KOTHE	Ja, ausgezeichnet. Danke.
OBER	Darf ich Ihnen noch etwas anbieten? Ein kleines Dessert?
HERR KOTHE	Ja, ich nehm' das Zitronensorbet Bellevue, bitte.
OBER	Ja, kommt sofort.

Put the meal on my bill, please.

HERR KOTHE	Herr Ober, schreiben Sie das Essen bitte mit auf meine Rechnung.
OBER	Welche Zimmernummer haben Sie?
HERR KOTHE	Nummer fünfundsiebzig.
OBER	Kleinen Moment, bitte . . . *(he brings the bill)* Bitte schön, ich brauch' eine Unterschrift.

AT THE RESTAURANT

In the restaurant Überseebrücke. *What's the soup of the*
day?

FR. HARRINGTON	Die Tagessuppe, was ist das heute?
OBER	Das ist eine Hamburger Krabbensuppe.

FR. HARRINGTON	Das klingt gut. Die möcht' ich gern.
OBER	Ja, gerne.

In the restaurant Schifferbörse. *What would you recommend today?*

HERR HINZE	Was würden Sie uns denn heute empfehlen?
OBER	Möchten Sie Fisch oder Fleisch?
FRAU EVRAHR	Also, ich nehme gerne Fisch.
OBER	Da hab' ich ein sehr schönes Heilbuttsteak, gebraten, mit Zitronenbutter, Kopfsalat und Dillkartoffeln.
FRAU EVRAHR	Das nehme ich.
OBER	Gerne. Und für den Herrn, bitte?
HERR HINZE	Ich hätte gerne Fleisch.
OBER	Ja, da hab' ich einen sehr schönen Schifferbörsentopf.
HERR HINZE	Was ist das, bitte?
OBER	Das sind drei verschiedene Filets.
HERR HINZE	Mit frischem Gemüse, Champignons, auf Bratkartoffeln.
OBER	Ja.
HERR HINZE	Aha, dann möchte ich gerne den Schifferbörsentopf.

Enjoy your meal! Guten Appetit!

OBER	Ich wünsch' Ihnen einen guten Appetit.
FRAU EVRAHR	Vielen Dank.
OBER	Bitte.
HERR HINZE	*(to Frau Evrahr)* Ja, guten Appetit!
FRAU EVRAHR	Ja, danke. Gleichfalls.

The bill, please! Keep the change!

HERR HINZE	Herr Ober! Die Rechnung, bitte.
OBER	Ja, ich mach' Ihnen gleich die Rechnung fertig . . . *(bringing the bill)* Bitte schön.
HERR HINZE	Danke. Einen Moment. Bitte . . . *(puts the*

money and a tip on the plate) So, das stimmt so. Danke.

OBER   Ja. Vielen Dank.

WORD LIST

für mich	for me
der Herr	sir
die Dame	madam
das Frühstücksbüffet	breakfast buffet
sich daran bedienen	help yourself from it
bekommen Sie auch Kuchen?	are you having cake as well?
ich habe . . . bestellt	I've ordered . . .
die Himbeertorte	raspberry flan
geben Sie mir . . .	give me . . .
speisen	to eat, dine
vorab	to begin with
der Hauptgang	main course
und Sie trinken dazu?	and to drink with it?
glaube ich	I think
ich brauche . . .	I need . . .
der Fisch	fish
das Fleisch	meat
das Heilbuttsteak	halibut steak
gebraten	fried
der Kopfsalat	lettuce
die Dillkartoffeln (f. pl.)	potatoes with dill
verschieden	different
mit frischem Gemüse	with fresh vegetables
die Champignons (m. pl.)	mushrooms
die Bratkartoffeln (f. pl.)	fried potatoes
gleichfalls	the same to you
ich mache Ihnen . . . fertig	I'll prepare . . . for you

EXPLANATIONS

GETTING THE MENU

Ask for: *die Speisekarte, bitte*. Don't confuse it with *das Menü!* *Ein Menü* is a fixed-price set meal. If you want a drink with your meal, ask for *die Weinkarte* or *die Getränkekarte*.

ORDERING

As with asking for things in shops, you can just say what you want and add *bitte*. Or you can start with *ich möchte* or *ich hätte gern* (I'd like) or *ich nehme* (I'll have):

ein Stück Apfelstrudel, bitte
ich hätte gern ein Glas Tee
ich möchte den Schifferbörsentopf
ich nehme einen trockenen Sherry

If what you order is a masculine word, you use *einen* or *den*.

For me and for you:
für mich ein Stück Nußtorte. Und für Sie?
To say what you'd like for a particular course use *als:*
als Vorspeise hätte ich gern die Hamburger Krebssuppe
als Hauptgang, die Scholle, bitte
als Dessert nehme ich das Zitronensorbet
Asking for a recommendation:
was würden Sie heute empfehlen?
To find out what something is:
was ist das?

You'll need to understand what the waiter says. He may ask:
. . . what you'd like:

möchten Sie	*speisen?*
	vorab einen Aperitif trinken?
	Fisch oder Fleisch?

. . . if you've chosen:
haben Sie schon gewählt?
. . . whether you enjoyed it:
hat's Ihnen geschmeckt?
. . . if he can offer you anything else:
darf ich Ihnen noch etwas anbieten?
And he's almost sure to wish you:
guten Appetit!

SETTLING THE BILL

Asking for the bill: *die Rechnung, bitte!*
And you'll probably want to give a tip:
stimmt so! or *das ist für Sie*

ABOUT WORD ORDER

In a simple German sentence the verb is the second element
(though not necessarily the second word):
ich/nehme/gern Fleisch
als Vorspeise/hätte/ich gern die Hamburger Krebssuppe
da/hab'/ich ein sehr schönes Heilbuttsteak

The verb is also the second element in a question beginning
with a question word:
was/ist/das?
welche Zimmernummer/haben/Sie?

If there's no specific question word, the question usually starts
with a verb:
bekommen/Sie auch Kuchen?
möchten/Sie speisen?
haben/Sie schon gewählt?

EXERCISES

SORTING OUT THE MENU

Here are some headings and items you might find on the
menu. Which dishes in the right-hand column belong to
which headings on the left?

1 Fleisch

2 Getränke

3 Desserts

4 Warme u. kalte Vorspeisen

5 Suppen

6 Fischspezialitäten

a Frische Nordsee-Scholle

b Ungarische Gulaschsuppe

c Rumpsteak vom Grill

d Rheinwein

e Krabbencocktail

f Vanille-Eis mit heißer
Schokolade

ORDERING A MEAL

7 You're eating out and this is the menu *(overleaf)*.

OBER	Guten Tag, die Dame/der Herr. Haben Sie schon gewählt?
SIE	(Order the Hamburg fish soup with garlic bread.)
OBER	Ja, gern. Und als Hauptgericht?
SIE	(As a main course you'll have North Sea plaice with Büsum★ prawns and parsley potatoes.)
OBER	Was trinken Sie dazu, bitte?
SIE	(You'd like a Rhine wine.)
OBER	Sehr gern. Haben Sie schon ein Dessert gewählt?
SIE	(Yes. Hot raspberries with vanilla ice cream and cream, please.)
OBER	Vielen Dank.

★ Büsum: resort and fishing centre on the North Sea coast, north of the Elbe.

Restaurant im Keller

Speisekarte

KALTE UND WARME VORSPEISEN
Knackfrischer Salat 6,50 DM
Forellenfilet mit Sahnemeerrettich, Toast und Butter 8,50 DM
Krabbencocktail 17,50 DM

SUPPEN
Tagessuppe 6,50 DM   *Hamburger Krabbensuppe 8,50 DM*
Ungarische Gulaschsuppe 7,50 DM   *Hamburger Fischsuppe mit Knoblauchbrot 9,00 DM*

FISCH
Schollenfilet mit Champignons, Artischoken und Butterkartoffeln 19,50 DM
Nordseescholle mit Büsumer Krabben und Petersilienkartoffeln 26,50 DM
Lachssteak vom Grill mit Tomaten, Champignons und Dillkartoffeln 29,50 DM
Seezungenfilet mit zerlassener Butter, Salzkartoffeln und Salatteller 41,50 DM

FLEISCH
Hamburger Labskaus, pikante Beilagen 16,50 DM
Lammfilets auf Knoblauchsauce, Blattspinat und Butterkartoffeln 21,50 DM
Kapitänspfanne mit drei kleinen Steaks, frischem Gemüse und Butterkartoffeln 23,50 DM
Pfeffersteak mit Petersilienkartoffeln und Salaten der Saison 36,50 DM

DESSERTS
Gemischtes Eis mit Sahne 6,50 DM   *Eiscafé mit Sahne 6,50 DM*
Heiße Himbeeren mit Vanille-Eis und Sahne 9,50 DM

SCHOPPENWEINE
Rhein 0,2l   7,50 DM   *Rotwein 0,2l   7,50 DM*
Mosel 0,2l   7,50 DM   *Franken 0,2l 9,50 DM*   *Rosé 0,2l   7,50 DM*

Preise verstehen sich incl. Bedienung und Mehrwertsteuer

PAYING BY CREDIT CARD

8   You've finished your meal and want to pay by credit card.

OBER	Hat es Ihnen geschmeckt?
SIE	(You found it excellent. And ask for the bill.)
OBER	Ja, gerne. Ich mache Ihnen sofort die Rechnung fertig.
SIE	(You want to pay, *bezahlen*, by credit card.)
OBER	Ja, gerne. Bitte, einen Moment . . . *(takes the card, returns with the slip)* Darf ich Sie bitten, hier zu unterschreiben?
SIE	(Yes, certainly. And give him a tip, saying, 'And that's for you.')
OBER	Vielen Dank. Auf Wiedersehen.
SIE	(Goodbye.)

9   Make out the bill by copying from the menu the dishes you had with their prices. What does that come to – in German?

COFFEE AND CAKE

10   Later you go to a café for *Kaffee und Kuchen*.

OBER	Ja, bitte?
SIE	(Coffee and a piece of lemon gateau, please.)
OBER	Ein Kännchen oder eine Tasse Kaffee?
SIE	(A cup, please.)
OBER	Und die Zitronentorte mit oder ohne Sahne?
SIE	(With cream.)
OBER	Gerne. Kommt sofort.

WORTH KNOWING

BREAKFAST

In hotels a set breakfast usually consists of various kinds of bread, rolls and preserves, sliced cheese, cold meats and sausage and perhaps a boiled egg (though many hotels now offer a breakfast of your choice from a breakfast buffet). Breakfast may or may not be included in the room price. To find out, ask: *ist das mit Frühstück?*

A GLASS OF TEA, A CUP OF COFFEE

As mentioned earlier, tea in a German restaurant or café can be quite expensive. So, instead of a pot, people often order just a glass. (There's even a special size of teabag, *die Glasportion*.) You'll never get a single *cup* of tea in a German restaurant, but you can order a cup of coffee. Restaurants sometimes refuse to serve a single glass of tea or a single cup

of coffee on weekends or holidays, or outside on the terrace.
Then you have to order a – more expensive – pot.

'CAKE TICKETS'

Most cafés display their gateaux, pastries and cakes at a glass-
covered counter, from which you make your choice. The
counter assistant will give you one part of a numbered chit,
rather like a cloakroom ticket. The other half goes onto the
plate with the cake you've chosen. The waitress at the table
will collect your half of the ticket and serve the matching cake
together with your drink.

HAMBURGER KREBSSUPPE

Many towns and cities have their own local specialities. In
Hamburg these include *Hamburger Krebssuppe* (crayfish soup)
or *Hamburger Aalsuppe* (eel soup). If you prefer something
more substantial, try *Finkenwerder Ewerscholle,* locally caught
plaice served with bacon, or *Labskaus,* a traditional sailor's
dish made from mashed potatoes with corned beef, herring,
beetroot and a fried egg.

CALLING THE WAITER OR WAITRESS

Calling a waiter is easy. Just say: *Herr Ober!* In a pub – and if
you're sure he's the landlord himself – you can call him:
Herr Wirt.

It used to be customary to call the waitress *Fräulein,* but today
waitresses increasingly resent this form of address, which was
originally used only for unmarried women. So, to be on the
safe side, just say: *Hallo!* Or indicate with your hand that
you want her attention.

GUTEN APPETIT!

People will wish you *guten Appetit!* both in restaurants and at family meals. Sometimes saying it indicates the official beginning of the meal.

RUHETAG

Most restaurants are closed for one day a week. This is usually indicated by a sign, *Ruhetag* (rest day) on the door.

TIPPING

Although service is included in prices at hotels and restaurants, waiters normally expect about 10 per cent of the charge as a tip. You can either hand the waiter the sum including the tip and say: *stimmt so* (that's all right) or, if you have no small change or are paying by credit card, you can simply say how much you want to pay, including tip. For example, with a bill of 36,50 DM, you might say: *vierzig Mark*. If you give the tip separately, say: *das ist für Sie* (that's for you), or you can just leave some money on the plate.

6 DOWN TO BUSINESS

KEY WORDS AND PHRASES

PEOPLE'S JOBS

was sind Sie von Beruf?	what's your job?
wo arbeiten Sie?	where do you work?
ich bin Ingenieur	I'm an engineer
ich arbeite bei (der Firma) Siemens	I work at Siemens

ARRANGING A MEETING

geht es . . .	is it possible . . .
morgen früh?	tomorrow morning?
um elf?	at eleven?
am Donnerstag nachmittag?	on Thursday afternoon?
das geht (nicht)	that's (not) possible

ARRIVING FOR AN APPOINTMENT

ich habe um 14 Uhr einen Termin bei Herrn Seel	I've an appointment with Herr Seel at 2 o'clock

TELEPHONING

ich möchte Herrn Gehrels sprechen	I'd like to speak to Herr Gehrels
ich rufe gegen zehn Uhr wieder an	I'll call back again at about ten

SOCIALISING

sind Sie verheiratet?	are you married?
haben Sie Kinder?	have you got children?
wie heißen sie?	what are their names?
wie alt sind sie?	how old are they?

CONVERSATIONS

The conversations in this chapter were recorded in Hamburg and in other cities.

PEOPLE'S JOBS

In Munich. I'm an engineer. I work at Neuberger Meßinstrumente Ltd.

HR. V. STETTEN	Wie ist Ihr Name, bitte?
HERR HOLZNER	Mein Name ist Gerd Holzner.
HR. V. STETTEN	Und woher kommen Sie?
HERR HOLZNER	Aus München.
HR. V. STETTEN	Was sind Sie von Beruf?
HERR HOLZNER	Ich bin Ingenieur.
HR. V. STETTEN	Und wo arbeiten Sie?
HERR HOLZNER	Ich arbeite bei der Firma Neuberger Meßinstrumente GmbH.

At Polyband, Munich. This is my marketing manager, this is my product manager.

HERR WINKEL	Das ist mein Marketingmanager, Herr Dünker . . .
HERR HUBER	Grüß Gott.
HERR DÜNKER	Herr Huber, grüß Gott.
HERR WINKEL	Und mein Produktmanager, Herr Bergheim.
HERR BERGHEIM	Grüß Gott, Herr Huber.
HERR HUBER	Grüß Gott, Herr Bergheim.

APPOINTMENTS
· ·

I need a haircut. Preferably tomorrow morning. Is it possible at eleven?

FR. HARRINGTON	Ich brauche einen neuen Haarschnitt, waschen und fönen.
FRAU RADTKE	Wann möchten Sie kommen?
FR. HARRINGTON	Am liebsten morgen früh.
FRAU RADTKE	Um zehn?
FR. HARRINGTON	Geht es auch um elf?
FRAU RADTKE	Es geht auch um elf.
FR. HARRINGTON	Ja, gut. Machen wir das.
FRAU RADTKE	Dann trag' ich Sie um elf Uhr ein.
FR. HARRINGTON	Okay. Bis dann.

At Polyband, Munich. I'd like to have a product meeting on Thursday afternoon. Is that all right with you?

HERR BERGHEIM	Herr Dünker, ich möchte gerne ein Produktmeeting machen, am Donnerstag nachmittag. Geht das bei Ihnen?
HERR DÜNKER	Moment, da muß ich erstmal nachsehen . . . Donnerstag nicht, aber es ginge am Freitag vormittag.
HERR BERGHEIM	Um neun Uhr?
HERR DÜNKER	Um neun Uhr . . . Ja, um neun Uhr ist in Ordnung.

At Audi, Ingolstadt. I've an appointment with Herr Seel at 2 o'clock.

HR. V. STETTEN	Grüß Gott!
PFÖRTNER	Grüß Gott!
HR. V. STETTEN	Mein Name ist von Stetten. Ich komm' aus London. Ich hab' um vierzehn Uhr einen Termin bei Herrn Seel.
PFÖRTNER	Moment, bitte, Herr von Stetten. Ich melde

	Sie an, ja? Moment, bitte.
HR. V. STETTEN	Gut. Danke.

TELEPHONING

At Lufthansa, Hamburg. What's your telephone number? I have a direct line . . . The code for Hamburg is 040.

HERR BESSEN	Wie ist Ihr Name, bitte?
HR. FÜSSINGER	Mein Name ist Peter Füssinger.
HERR BESSEN	Und Ihre Telefonnummer hier in der Firma bei der Lufthansa?
HR. FÜSSINGER	Ich habe eine Durchwahlnummer; die ist fünf null neun zwei fünf sieben drei.
HERR BESSEN	Und die Vorwahlnummer von Hamburg?
HR. FÜSSINGER	Die Vorwahl ist null vier null.

At Pringle, Düsseldorf. Excuse me, what was your name again? And your telephone number?

HR. PERLBACH	Entschuldigung, wie war nochmal Ihr Name?
FRAU PAESCH	Paesch.
HR. PERLBACH	Und Ihre Telefonnummer?
FRAU PAESCH	Siebenunddreißig . . .
HR. PERLBACH	Siebenunddreißig . . .
FRAU PAESCH	Vierzig . . .
HR. PERLBACH	Vierzig . . .
FRAU PAESCH	Sechsundzwanzig . . .
HR. PERLBACH	Sechsundzwanzig. Danke schön.

This is Siemens, London. Is Herr Paulig in the office?

FRAU PIELKE	*(answering the phone)* Siemens AG, Sekretariat Herr Mehloch. Guten Tag.
FRAU BLUM	Hier Siemens London, Frau Blum. Guten Tag. Ist Herr Paulig im Büro?
FRAU PIELKE	Der Herr Paulig ist da. Darf ich Sie

	verbinden, Frau Blum?
FRAU BLUM	Ja, bitte.
FRAU PIELKE	Kleinen Moment, ich stell' Sie durch.
FRAU BLUM	Danke.
FRAU PIELKE	Auf Wiederhören.
FRAU BLUM	Wiederhören.

I'd like to speak to Herr Gehrels. When's the meeting over? Right, I'll call again then.

FRAU VERTIC	Siemens AG, das Büro von Herrn Gehrels. Guten Morgen.
FRAU BLUM	Guten Tag. Siemens London, Frau Blum hier. Ich möchte gerne Herrn Gehrels sprechen.
FRAU VERTIC	Oh, das tut mir leid. Herr Gehrels ist in einer Besprechung.
FRAU BLUM	Wann ist denn die Besprechung zu Ende?
FRAU VERTIC	So gegen zehn Uhr.
FRAU BLUM	Ja, gut, dann ruf' ich gegen zehn Uhr wieder an.

SOCIALISING

Are you married? Yes, I have two sons and a small daughter.

FRAU PAGITZ	Herr Göttsch, sind Sie verheiratet?
DR. GÖTTSCH	Ja.
FRAU PAGITZ	Und haben Sie Kinder?
DR. GÖTTSCH	Ja, ich habe zwei Söhne und eine kleine Tochter.
FRAU PAGITZ	Und wie heißen sie?
DR. GÖTTSCH	Meine Söhne heißen Peter und Klaus, und das Mädchen heißt Karin.
FRAU PAGITZ	Und wie alt sind die Kinder?
DR. GÖTTSCH	Peter ist fünfzehn, Klaus ist acht, und Karin ist gerade drei Monate alt.

WORD LIST

der Ingenieur	engineer (with university degree)
die Firma	company
GmbH (Gesellschaft mit beschränkter Haftung)	Ltd
waschen und föhnen	wash and blow dry
machen wir das	let's do that
ich trag' Sie ein	I'll put you down
bis dann	till then
ich muß nachsehen	I must have a look
erstmal	first
bei Ihnen	for/with you
es ginge	it would be possible
der Pförtner	porter
ich melde Sie an	I'll tell them you're here
die ist . . .	it is . . .
zwo = zwei	two
verbinden	to connect
ich stell' Sie durch	I'll put you through
AG (Aktiengesellschaft)	plc
die Besprechung	meeting
das Mädchen	girl
gerade	just
drei Monate	three months

EXPLANATIONS

WHAT'S YOUR JOB?

In English you say, 'I'm an engineer, I'm a representative', but in German you don't need a word for 'a' or 'an'. You just say: *ich bin Ingenieur, ich bin Vertreter*

Many (though not all) female occupations end with -in:

	MASCULINE	FEMININE
doctor	*Arzt*	*Ärztin*
export manager	*Exportleiter*	*Exportleiterin*
teacher	*Lehrer*	*Lehrerin*
taxi driver	*Taxifahrer*	*Taxifahrerin*
shop assistant	*Verkäufer*	*Verkäuferin*
representative	*Vertreter*	*Vertreterin*

WHERE DO YOU WORK?

To say where you work use *bei*; to say which company you're from use *von*:

ich arbeite bei (der Firma) Neuberger Meßinstrumente
ich bin von (der) Firma Polyband

Although it's *die Firma*, after *bei* und *von*, *die* changes to *der*. In the same way *der* and *das* change to *dem*. The same happens after *aus*, *mit*, *nach* and *zu*:

kommt etwas aus der Minibar dazu?
fahren Sie mit dem Auto?
wie komme ich zur (= zu der) Ost-West-Straße?
nach dem Frühstück machen wir eine Stadtrundfahrt

TIMES OF DAY

yesterday	*gestern*	morning	*der Vormittag*
today	*heute*	afternoon	*der Nachmittag*
tomorrow	*morgen*	evening	*der Abend*

So:

10 a.m.	*zehn Uhr vormittags*
10 p.m.	*zehn Uhr abends*
yesterday afternoon	*gestern nachmittag*
this evening	*heute abend*

tomorrow morning   *morgen vormittag* (or, like Frau
                     Harrington, you can say: *morgen früh*)

ICH MÖCHTE GERNE . . . SPRECHEN

A small group of verbs (called modal verbs) are not complete
on their own. They almost always need another verb to
complete them:
ich **möchte** *gerne Herrn Gehrels* **sprechen**
darf *ich Sie* **verbinden**?
da **muß** *ich erst* **nachsehen.**
kann *ich Ihnen* **helfen**?

WIE HEISSEN SIE?

Sie (with a capital letter) means 'you', but *sie* (with a small
letter) means 'they'. So Frau Pagitz' question asking the
names of Dr. Göttsch's children is written: *wie heißen sie?*
With a small letter, *sie* can also mean 'she' or, if you are
referring to a feminine noun, 'it'. The word for 'he', or 'it' if
you're referring to a masculine noun, is *er*.

ABOUT VERBS

When you look up a verb in a dictionary, you usually find the
'infinitive', e.g. *gehen* to go, *kommen* to come, *heißen* to be
called. From this you can work out the various parts of the
verb. With *ich* the ending is usually -*e*, with *er* (he/it), *sie* (she/
it) and *es* (it) it's usually -*t* and with *wir* (we), *Sie* (you) and *sie*
(they), -*en:*

	gehen (to go)	*kommen* (to come)	*heißen* (to be called)
ich	*gehe*	*komme*	*heiße*
er, sie, es	*geht*	*kommt*	*heißt*
wir, Sie, sie	*gehen*	*kommen*	*heißen*

There are, of course, exceptions. Among them the two most common verbs of all:

	sein	*haben*
	(to be)	(to have)
ich	*bin*	*habe*
er, sie es	*ist*	*hat*
wir, Sie, sie	*sind*	*haben*

EXERCISES

APPOINTMENTS

1   These diary entries might have been made by the people in the recordings. Fill them in on the diary page and add the times. Today is Tuesday! Times in German are written like this: 8 o'clock – *8h;* 11.30 – *11.30h.*

TERMINE IN DIESER WOCHE	
MONTAG	
DIENSTAG	
MITTWOCH	
DONNERSTAG	
FREITAG	
SONNABEND	
SONNTAG	

FRAU HARRINGTON	Friseur
HERR BERGHEIM	Produktmeeting, Herr Dünker
HERR VON STETTEN	Audi, Herr Seel
SIE (see Exercise 4)	Mercedes, Herr Tasche

DIRECTORY ENQUIRIES

2   You want to make a call to Mercedes-Benz. You ring directory inquiries, *die Auskunft, (elf achtundachtzig)* to ask for the number.

AUSKUNFT	*(answering the phone)* Auskunft, Platz dreizehn.* Guten Tag.
SIE	(Hello, you'd like the number of Mercedes-Benz in Stuttgart.)
AUSKUNFT	Einen Moment bitte. Ja, hier hab' ich sie: siebenundvierzig, dreiundfünfzig, null.
SIE	(And what's the code for Stuttgart?)
AUSKUNFT	Die Vorwahl ist null, sieben, elf.
SIE	(Thank you and goodbye.)
AUSKUNFT	Wiederhör'n.

*Directory enquiries give the seat number, so that you can trace who you've spoken to.

GETTING THROUGH

3 You ring Mercedes-Benz.

FRAU SCHMIDT	*(answering the phone)* Mercedes-Benz, Stuttgart. Schmidt, guten Tag.
SIE	(Greet her and say you'd like to speak to the personnel manager, *den Personalchef*.)
FRAU SCHMIDT	Es tut mir leid, aber Herr Tasche ist in einer Konferenz. Kann ich ihm etwas ausrichten, *give him a message?*
SIE	(No, thanks. Ask when the meeting will be over.)
FRAU SCHMIDT	Ich denke, so gegen vierzehn Uhr.
SIE	(Fine, you'll call again at about 2 o'clock.)
FRAU SCHMIDT	Gut. Herr Tasche hat eine Durchwahl-nummer: siebenundvierzig, dreiundfünfzig, achtunddreißig, zwölf.
SIE	(Repeat the number in English as you write it down. Then say thank you and goodbye.)
FRAU SCHMIDT	Danke für Ihren Anruf. Auf Wiederhören.

FIXING A TIME

4   At 2 o'clock you ring again and get through.

SIE   (Tell Herr Tasche you'd like to visit, *besuchen,* him. And ask if it's possible on Friday afternoon.)

HERR TASCHE   Einen Moment, bitte. Da muß ich erst im Terminkalender nachsehen . . . Tja, Freitag ist schlecht, aber Sonnabend vormittag ginge es.

SIE   (Ask if it would be possible at 10.30.)

HERR TASCHE   Ja gut, um halb elf ist in Ordnung.

ARRIVING FOR AN APPOINTMENT

5   You arrive on Saturday at 10.30. Greet the porter and say you have an appointment. Tell him what time it is and who it's with.

PFÖRTNER   Guten Morgen. Kann ich Ihnen helfen?

SIE   _____ .

PFÖRTNER   Augenblick bitte, ich melde Sie eben an.

SIE   (Thank him.)

PERSONAL DETAILS

6   Over a cup of coffee after the meeting you have a chat. You're married with one son James, who's 16 years old. What do you tell Herr Tasche?

HERR TASCHE   Sagen Sie, sind Sie verheiratet?

SIE   _____ .

HERR TASCHE   Und haben Sie Kinder?

SIE   _____ .

HERR TASCHE   Wie heißt er denn?

SIE   _____ .

HERR TASCHE   Und wie alt ist James?

SIE   _____ .

HERR TASCHE	Ich würde Sie gern mal besuchen. Ich bin nächste Woche in London. Sagen Sie, wie ist Ihre Telefonnummer?
SIE	(3 57 65 19. Try it in pairs!)
HERR TASCHE	Und die Vorwahl?
SIE	(071)
HERR TASCHE	Gut, dann ruf' ich Sie an, wenn ich in London bin. Bis dann!

DIRECTORY ENQUIRIES AGAIN

7 You have to ring computer companies in different German cities to obtain quotations. You ring directory enquiries again and get the following information. Fill it in on the address page below.

ANSCHRIFTEN		
FIRMA	**ORT**	**TELEFON**

IBM, Stuttgart
null einhundertdreißig*/fünfundvierzig, siebenundsechzig

Panasonic, Hamburg
null vierzig/fünfundachtzig, neunundvierzig, siebenundzwanzig, sechsundsiebzig

Tandon Computer GmbH, Frankfurt/Main
null neunundsechzig/vier, zwanzig, fünfundneunzig, einhundertdreiundachtzig

Laser Computer GmbH, Düsseldorf
null, zwo, elf/neunundfünfzig, achtundvierzig,
dreiundneunzig

NEC Deutschland GmbH, München
null, neunundachtzig/neun, dreißig, null, sechs, null

Epson Deutschland GmbH, Düsseldorf
null, zwo, elf/sechsundfünfzig, null, drei, null

Plantron Computer GmbH, Bad Homburg
null, einundsechzig, zweiundsiebzig/fünfundzwanzig,
einhundertachtundachtzig

*null einhundertdreißig is a free-phone number like 0800 in Great Britain!

<hr>

WORTH KNOWING

ENGINEERS AND TECHNICIANS

In Germany an *Ingenieur* has studied at a university
(*Diplomingenieur*) or at a technical college (*graduierter
Ingenieur*). All other engineers are called *Techniker*
(technicians).

TELEPHONE NUMBERS

Like Frau Paesch, people often give their telephone numbers
in pairs:
siebenunddreißig, vierzig, sechsundzwanzig
This is also the way they're listed in the telephone directory:
37 40 26
If an odd figure is left over, it looks and sounds like this:
7 84 67, *sieben, vierundachtzig, siebenundsechzig*.
If the number is short, it can be grouped in hundreds: 0 130/
324 would be *null, einhundertdreißig/dreihundertvierundzwanzig*.

People often say *zwo* instead of *zwei:*

zwei	*zwo*
zweiundzwanzig	*zwoundzwanzig*
einhundertzwei	*einhundertzwo*

This is to avoid any confusion with *drei*.

TELEPHONING

Phone boxes throughout Germany are yellow, but will change to white in the near future. You need at least 30 pfennigs to make a call, or you can buy a phone card (12 DM for 40 units) from the post office. You can make international calls from most phone boxes.

Of course, you can call from your hotel as well, but it's likely to be expensive. A unit often costs twice as much as from a box or from the post office. As yet very few phone boxes can receive calls: a bell sign on the door indicates where they do.

Normal rates apply Mondays to Fridays from 8 a.m. to 6 p.m. At all other times telephoning, even internationally, is considerably cheaper.

German telephone signals are different from those in the UK and USA. When you lift the receiver you'll hear a continuous beeping sound. After dialling, the same sound with interruptions indicates that you're through. If you hear short *tüt-tüt-tüt* sounds, you'll know the line is engaged.

SENDING A FAX

If you want to use a fax machine, see if there's one in your hotel. From there it will be much cheaper than from the post office. The hotel will charge you by the unit, while at the post office you pay a very high fixed rate for each page.

CAN YOU *GET BY* ?

Try this section when you've finished the course. If you get it all right you should be able to *Get by!*

MEETING PEOPLE

1 You arrive in Hamburg at 9.30 a.m. and a friend has come to meet you. How do you greet him?
a Guten Morgen
b Guten Tag
c Guten Abend
d Auf Wiedersehen

2 You haven't met his wife, so you introduce yourself to her: _____ .

3 Then you ask her what her name is: _____ ?

4 She asks you: *Wie geht es Ihnen?*
What do you say after enjoying a smooth flight from London to Hamburg? _____ .

5 She asks you: *Woher kommen Sie?*
She wants to know:
a where you're going
b where you're from

c where you're staying
d when you're leaving
e how long you're staying

6 You all go into a pub for a drink. You order. Your friend wants a pot of coffee, his wife would like a coke and you want to try the famous German beer. What do you say to the waiter? _____ .

7 When you order the beer the waiter asks you: *Ein großes oder ein kleines?*
Does that mean:
a a warm or cold one?
b a large or small one?
c a light or dark one?
d a bitter or a lager?

SHOPPING

8 Next morning you go out to do some shopping. At the supermarket you want 100g of Dutch cheese. What do you say?
a Ein Pfund Holländer,
b Zweihundert Gramm Holländer,
c Hundert Gramm Schweizer,   bitte.
d Hundert Gramm Holländer,
e Zweihundert Gramm Engländer,

9 At a market stall you decide to buy a kilo of tomatoes and three bananas. What do you say? _____ .

10 At the post office you ask how much the postage is for a postcard to the UK. Then you buy three stamps:

SIE   _____ .

BEAMTER   Eine Postkarte nach Großbritannien kostet
                   sechzig Pfennig.

SIE   _____ .

11   At the bank you want to cash a cheque. You need
350,– DM. You have to write the sum in words:

_____ Deutsche Mark

12   The bank clerk tells you: *Bitte unterschreiben Sie hier.*
Does he want you to:
a   write in the amount of money you want?
b   write in the date?
c   write in your name in block letters?
d   sign your name here?
e   write in your address?

FINDING SOMEWHERE TO STAY

13   A few days later you travel south to Munich. You've
booked a room in advance at the Münchener Hof. When you
arrive there, what do you say?
a   Ich möchte ein Zimmer reservieren.
b   Haben Sie ein Zimmer frei?
c   Ich habe ein Zimmer reserviert.

14   The girl at reception can't remember what kind of room
you've booked. You want a single room with bath. What do
you say?
a   Ein Doppelzimmer mit Bad, bitte.
b   Ein Einzelzimmer mit Dusche, bitte.
c   Ein Einzelzimmer mit Bad, bitte.
d   Ein Doppelzimmer mit Dusche, bitte.

15   The receptionist tells you: *Mit Frühstück macht das fünfundachtzig Mark pro Nacht*.
The room costs:
a   85,– DM with breakfast
b   58,– DM with breakfast
c   85,– DM without breakfast
d   58,– DM without breakfast

16   You need a taxi and ring reception to ask for one. Your room number is 97.

SIE   _____ .

EMPFANG   Ja, sicher. Wie ist, bitte, Ihre Zimmernummer?

SIE   _____ .

GETTING ABOUT

17   The taxi takes you right into the city. As you need some medicine, you ask the taxi-driver where you can find a pharmacy. What do you say?
Wo gibt es hier . . .
a   eine Bank?
b   ein Postamt?
c   eine Apotheke?
d   eine Bushaltestelle?
e   eine Kunsthalle?

18   The pharmacy is in the pedestrian precinct, so the driver drops you off and gives you directions:
Sie gehen hier geradeaus, dann rechts und dann gleich die zweite Straße links. Sie ist dann auf der linken Seite.
Where do you go?
a   right/next right/third left/it's on the right
b   straight on/right/second left/it's on the left
c   straight on/left/second right/it's on the right
d   left/right/first left/it's on the left

19   Next you want to visit Munich's famous art gallery, *die Pinakothek*. You ask a passer-by the best way to get there:

_____ ?

20   You want to know how long it will take you on foot:

_____ ?

21   It would take half an hour so you decide to go by bus. You ask how long that would take: _____ ?

22   Next, you ask where the nearest bus-stop is:

_____ ?

23   You are told: *Die Haltestelle ist gleich hier um die Ecke.*
Is the bus-stop:
a   right in front of you?
b   right behind you?
c   straight ahead?
d   just round the corner?
e   a long way from here?

EATING OUT

24   After your visit to the art gallery you feel really hungry and go into a restaurant for a meal. You call the waiter and ask for the menu: _____ !

Before the meal you drink a sherry (**25**). You want to have a soup (**26**) as a starter, a good helping of meat (**27**) for the main course and an ice cream (**28**) for dessert. You'd like to drink red wine (**29**) with your meal and a cup of coffee (**30**) afterwards.
Under which sections of the menu would you find them?

a Vorspeisen
b Suppen
c Fleischgerichte
d Fischspezialitäten
e Nachspeisen
f Eiskarte
g Biere
h Weine
i Aperitifs und Schnäpse
j alkoholfreie Getränke
k heiße Getränke

31 As you have problems in understanding the menu, you ask the waiter what he'd recommend: _____ ?

32 You don't know what that is either, so you ask:
_____ ?

33 You decide to follow the waiter's recommendation and have the dish. What do you say? _____ .

34 When the waiter serves the meal he says: *Guten Appetit!* That means:
a enjoy your meal
b anything else?
c please pay now
d please hurry up

35 After the meal you ask for the bill. What do you say?
_____ .

36 The waiter tells you: *Das macht sechsundfünfzig Mark fünfzig*. What's that in figures? _____ DM

37   You pay with a hundred mark note. What does the waiter say as he gives you your change?
Bitte sehr . . .
a   vierunddreißig Mark fünfzig zurück
b   einundvierzig Mark fünfzig zurück
c   zweiundfünfzig Mark fünfzig zurück
d   dreiundvierzig Mark fünfzig zurück

38   Do you remember the German currency denominations? What are the fewest notes and coins you can expect as change?

_____ .

39   After you've received your change you give the waiter a tip. What do you say?
a   stimmt so!
b   das ist für Sie!

DOWN TO BUSINESS

40   Next day you ring the computer company NEC in Munich to arrange an appointment with the sales manager (*der Verkaufsleiter*). What do you say?
a   Wie ist Ihre Telefonnummer bei der Firma NEC?
b   Ich habe einen Termin beim Verkaufsleiter.
c   Ich möchte, bitte, den Verkaufsleiter sprechen.

41   He's not there but his secretary gives you the number of his direct line: *neunhundertdreißig, null, sechs, vierhundertfünf.*
You write it down in figures: _____ .

42   She also asks you: *Ginge es heute vormittag?*
What does she want to know?
Would it be all right . . .

a   this afternoon?
b   tomorrow morning?
c   this morning?
d   tomorrow afternoon?
e   this lunchtime?

43   You make an appointment with Herr Fischer for 11. At the NEC reception you are greeted by the porter. You introduce yourself, and tell him where you come from (Joy Computers, London), the time of your appointment and who it's with. What do you say? _____ .

44   After the meeting Herr Fischer asks you a few personal questions. You're an import manager (*der Importleiter*) at Joy Computers, and are married with three children, Mary (3), Jane (7) and Gordon (11). What are your answers?

HERR FISCHER   Was sind Sie von Beruf?

SIE   _____ .

HERR FISCHER   Und wo arbeiten Sie?

SIE   _____ .

HERR FISCHER   Sind Sie verheiratet?

SIE   _____ .

HERR FISCHER   Haben Sie auch Kinder?

SIE   _____ .

HERR FISCHER   Und wie heißen sie?

SIE   _____ .

HERR FISCHER   Wie alt sind denn die Kinder?

SIE   _____ .

REFERENCE SECTION

German pronunciation isn't really difficult. The best way to get it right is to listen carefully to the cassettes and copy what you hear as closely as possible. This pronunciation guide is recorded at the end of the second cassette with pauses for you to repeat the words. Go through it as often as you like until you feel really confident.

VOWELS

Vowels can be long or short. Double vowels are long, as in *Tee, Kaffee*. And vowels are long before an *h*, as in *gehen*. Before a double consonant they're short, as in *Herr, Zimmer*.

a	long	*Sahne, haben*
	or short	*danke, Flasche*
e	long	*gehen, Bremen*
	or short	*gern, Herr*
i	long	*Ihnen, Kilo*
	or short	*bitte, ist*
o	long	*groß, oder*
	or short	*kommen, kostet*
u	long	*gut, Dusche*
	or short	*zum, Pfund*

VOWELS WITH *UMLAUTS*

These have no English equivalents. Listen to the cassette and copy the pronunciation as closely as you can.

ä	long	*Käse, ungefähr*
	or short	*Kännchen, Äpfel*
ö	long	*schön*
	or short	*möchte*
ü	long	*für, Menü*
	or short	*fünf, Stück*

VOWEL COMBINATIONS

au	like 'ow' in 'how'	*Frau, aus*
ai ⎫ ei ⎭	like 'y' in 'my'	*Mai* *Wein*
ie	like 'ee' in 'tree'	*die, hier*
äu ⎫ eu ⎭	like 'oy' in 'toy'	*Fräulein* *Deutsch*

CONSONANTS

Most sound similar to English, but there are some points to notice.

ch	after *a, o, u* and *au* like 'ch' in the Scottish 'loch'.	*macht, noch* *Kuchen, auch*
	Otherwise like 'h' in huge	*ich, rechts*
chs	like 'x' in 'sex'	*sechs*
d	at the end of a word like 't'	*Bad*
-ig	at the end of a word, usually as in *ich*	*zwanzig*
j	like 'y' in 'you'	*ja, Jahr*
r	rolled from the back of the throat	*rot, rechts*
sch	like 'sh' in 'shop'	*Schlüssel, Flasche*
sp	at the beginning of a word, 'shp'	*Speisekarte, sprechen*

st	at the beginning of a word, 'sht'	*Stück, Straße*
v	like 'f' in 'for'	*vier, von*
w	like 'v' in 'vine'	*weit, auf Wiedersehen*
z	like 'ts' in 'cats'	*zehn, zu*

NUMBERS

0	*null*	10	*zehn*	20	*zwanzig*
1	*eins*	11	*elf*	21	*einundzwanzig*
2	*zwei*	12	*zwölf*	22	*zweiundzwanzig*
3	*drei*	13	*dreizehn*	23	*dreiundzwanzig*
4	*vier*	14	*vierzehn*	24	*vierundzwanzig*
5	*fünf*	15	*fünfzehn*	25	*fünfundzwanzig*
6	*sechs*	16	*sechzehn*	26	*sechsundzwanzig*
7	*sieben*	17	*siebzehn*	27	*siebenundzwanzig*
8	*acht*	18	*achtzehn*	28	*achtundzwanzig*
9	*neun*	19	*neunzehn*	29	*neunundzwanzig*

30	*dreißig*	80	*achtzig*
40	*vierzig*	90	*neunzig*
50	*fünfzig*	100	*hundert*
60	*sechzig*	200	*zweihundert*
70	*siebzig*	1000	*tausend*

PRICES AND TIMES

These are usually written as follows:

Prices	35 DM	*fünfunddreißig Mark*
	2,58 DM	*zwei Mark achtundfünfzig*
Times	11.16 Uhr	*elf Uhr sechzehn*
	18.38 Uhr	*achtzehn Uhr achtunddreißig*

DAYS OF THE WEEK

Sonntag	Sunday	*Donnerstag*	Thursday
Montag	Monday	*Freitag*	Friday
Dienstag	Tuesday	*Samstag* or	Saturday
Mittwoch	Wednesday	*Sonnabend*	

MONTHS OF THE YEAR

Januar	January	*Juli*	July
Februar	February	*August*	August
März	March	*September*	September
April	April	*Oktober*	October
Mai	May	*November*	November
Juni	June	*Dezember*	December

KEY TO EXERCISES

1 MEETING PEOPLE

HELLO AND GOODBYE

1a Guten Tag! **b** Guten Abend! **c** Hallo, Dieter.
d Tschüs, Dieter.

HOW ARE YOU?

2 Hallo (*or* Guten Tag), Herr Meier./Danke, gut./(wie geht es) Ihnen?/ Danke/gut.

WHERE ARE YOU FROM?

3 Nein, ich bin Schotte *or* Schottin./Aus Edinburgh? Nein, ich bin nicht aus Edinburgh!/Ich komme aus Glasgow.

ORDERING DRINKS

4 Herr Ober!/Ein Bier, bitte./Ein kleines, bitte./Einen Whisky./Mit Eis, bitte.

MORE DRINKS

5 Möchten Sie Kaffee?/Mit Zitrone oder Milch?/Nein, ich möchte Kaffee./Möchten Sie Tee?/Möchten Sie heiße Schokolade?/Eine große oder eine kleine Tasse?/Herr Ober!/ Ein Kännchen Tee, ein Kännchen Kaffee und eine große Tasse heiße Schokolade, bitte.

2 SHOPPING

YOUR SHOPPING LIST

1 Zwei Postkarten, bitte. Fünfhundert Gramm (*or* ein Pfund) Edamer, bitte. Acht Brötchen, bitte. Ein Paket Kekse, bitte. Fünf Rosen, bitte. Eine Flasche Rotwein, bitte. Ein Pfund Äpfel, bitte. Eine Tüte Milch, bitte. **2** 2,37 DM, 24,11 DM, 17,43 DM.

AT THE DELICATESSEN

3 Ich hätte gern (*or* ich möchte gern) dreihundert Gramm Holländer (*or* Dreihundert Gramm Holländer, bitte)./ Geschnitten, bitte./Vielen Dank (*or* Danke schön).

THE MARKET FRUIT STALL

4 Ein Kilo Tomaten, bitte./Ja, ein Pfund (*or* fünfhundert Gramm) Bananen, bitte./Haben Sie Kiwis?/Acht Stück, bitte. **5** 10,14 DM (zehn Mark und vierzehn).

AT THE POST OFFICE

6 Wieviel kostet ein Brief nach England?/Ich möchte drei Briefmarken, bitte./Haben Sie Postkarten?/Vier. Wieviel kostet eine (Postkarte)?/ Was macht das, bitte?/Bitte sehr (*or* Bitte schön)./Vielen Dank. Auf Wiedersehen. **7** Two 2 DM notes; two 2 DM coins; one 50 pfennig coin; and one 10 pfennig coin.

CASHING A TRAVELLER'S CHEQUE

8 Guten Tag. Ich möchte gern einen Reisescheck einlösen./ Hier?/Vielen Dank (*or* Danke schön). Auf Wiedersehen. **9** 396,50 DM **10** 3,50 DM.

3 FINDING SOMEWHERE TO STAY

TELEPHONING A HOTEL

1 Guten Tag. Ich hätte gern *or* ich möchte ein Einzelzimmer mit Dusche./Was (*or* wieviel) kostet das (Zimmer)?/Ach, nein danke (*or* Ach, das geht nicht). Auf Wiederhören.

AT THE TOURIST INFORMATION CENTRE

2 Ich möchte ein Zimmer reservieren./Ich hätte gern (*or* ich möchte) ein Einzelzimmer mit Dusche./(Für) vier Nächte, bitte./Was (*or* wieviel) kostet das (Zimmer)?/Ja, das nehme ich (*or* Ja, das geht).

CHECKING IN

3 Guten Tag. Mein Name ist . . . Ich habe ein Zimmer reserviert./Mit Dusche./Bitte schön./Können Sie mir ein Taxi bestellen?/Vielen Dank (*or* Danke schön).

ROOM SERVICE

4 Ich hätte gern (*or* ich möchte) eine Flasche Wein./Weißen, bitte./Ja, eine Flasche (Mineral) Wasser, bitte./Danke. Auf Wiederhören.

AT THE CAMP SITE

5 Haben Sie noch Zeltplätze frei?/Wir sind drei Erwachsene und ein Kind./Ja, ein Auto. Was (*or* wieviel) kosted das?/Ja, das geht.

4 GETTING ABOUT

GOING BY UNDERGROUND

1 (Entschuldigen Sie bitte,) wo ist die nächste U–Bahn Station? **2** (Entschuldigen Sie bitte,) welche Nummer fährt in die Innenstadt?

FINDING A CAFÉ

3 Entschuldigen Sie bitte, gibt es hier in der Nähe ein Café?/
Ist es weit (von hier)?

WHEN IS THE BANK OPEN?

5 Wann sind Ihre Öffnungszeiten?/Haben Sie samstags (*or*
sonnabends) geöffnet?

6

DEUTSCHE BANK, HAMBURG	
ÖFFNUNGSZEITEN:	
Mo./Di./Mi.:	9.00 Uhr bis 16.30 Uhr
Donnerstag:	9.00 Uhr bis 18.00 Uhr
Freitag:	9.00 Uhr bis 14.30 Uhr
Samstag:	geschlossen

7 Kleine Stadtrundfahrt mit Alster-Bootsfahrt.

5 EATING OUT

SORTING OUT THE MENU

1 c **2** d **3** f **4** e **5** b **6** a

ORDERING A MEAL

7 Ich hätte gern (*or* ich möchte bitte) die Hamburger Fischsuppe mit Knoblauchbrot. (*or* Die Hamburger Fischsuppe mit Knoblauchbrot, bitte.)/Als Hauptgang nehme ich die Nordseescholle mit Büsumer Krabben und Petersilienkartoffeln./Ich möchte (*or* ich hätte gern) einen Rheinwein, bitte./Ja, heiße Himbeeren mit Vanille-Eis und Sahne, bitte.

Menu

Menu

COLD AND WARM STARTERS
Salad – fresh from the field
Trout fillet with horseradish sauce, toast and butter
Prawn cocktail

SOUPS

Soup of the day *Hamburg prawn soup*
Hungarian goulash soup *Hamburg fish soup with garlic bread*

FISH
Plaice fillet with mushrooms, artichokes and butter potatoes
North Sea plaice with Büsum prawns and parsley potatoes
Salmon steak (grilled) with tomatoes, mushrooms and dill potatoes
Sole fillet with melted butter, boiled potatoes and mixed salad

MEAT
Hamburg Labskaus, tasty side dish
Lamb fillets in garlic sauce, spinach and butter potatoes
Captain's Plate with three small steaks, fresh vegetables and butter potatoes
Pepper steak with parsley potatoes and seasonal salad

DESSERTS
Mixed ice cream with cream *Ice-coffee with cream*
Hot raspberries with vanilla ice cream and cream

WINE (BY THE GLASS)

Rhine *Red wine*
Moselle *Franconian* *Rosé*

All prices include service and VAT!

PAYING BY CREDIT CARD

8 Ja, danke. Ausgezeichnet. Bitte, die Rechnung./Ich möchte mit Kreditkarte bezahlen./Ja, sicher. Und das ist für Sie./Auf Wiedersehen.

9

Hamburger Fischsuppe mit Knoblauchbrot:	9,00 DM
Nordseescholle mit Büsumer Krabben und Petersilienkartoffeln:	26,50 DM
Heiße Himbeeren mit Vanille-Eis und Sahne:	9,50 DM
Rheinwein:	7,50 DM
SUMME:	52,50 DM

COFFEE AND CAKE

10 Kaffee und ein Stück Zitronentorte, bitte./Eine Tasse, bitte./Mit Sahne (, bitte).

6 DOWN TO BUSINESS

APPOINTMENTS

1

TERMINE IN DIESER WOCHE	
MONTAG	
DIENSTAG	14h Audi, Herr Seel
MITTWOCH	11h Friseur
DONNERSTAG	
FREITAG	9h Produktmeeting, Herr Dünker
SONNABEND	10.30h Mercedes, Herr Tasche
SONNTAG	

DIRECTORY ENQUIRIES

2   Guten Tag. Ich hätte gern (*or* ich möchte gern) die
Nummer von Mercedes-Benz in Stuttgart./Und wie ist die
Vorwahl von Stuttgart?/Vielen Dank (*or* Danke schön). Auf
Wiederhören.

GETTING THROUGH

3   Guten Tag. Ich möchte gerne den Personalchef sprechen./
Nein, danke. Wann ist die Konferenz zu Ende?/Gut. Ich rufe
gegen vierzehn Uhr wieder an./47 53 38 12. Vielen Dank. Auf
Wiederhören.

FIXING A TIME

4   Guten Tag, Herr Tasche. Ich möchte Sie gern besuchen.
Geht es am Freitag nachmittag?/Ginge es um halb elf (*or* um
zehn Uhr dreißig)?

ARRIVING FOR AN APPOINTMENT

5   Guten Morgen. Ich habe um halb elf einen Termin bei
Herrn Tasche./Vielen Dank (*or* Danke schön).

PERSONAL DETAILS

6   Ja, ich bin verheiratet./Ja, (ich habe) einen Sohn./Er heißt
James./Er ist sechzehn./Drei, siebenundfünfzig,
fünfundsechzig, neunzehn./Null, einundsiebzig.

7	A N S C H R I F T E N		
FIRMA	**ORT**	**TELEFON**	
IBM	Stuttgart	0130-4567	
Panasonic	Hamburg	040-854927	
Tandon Computer GmbH	Frankfurt/Main	069-420 95183	
Laser Computer GmbH	Düsseldorf	0211-594893	
NEC Deutschland GmbH	München	089-930060	
Epson Deutschland GmbH	Düsseldorf	0211-56030	
Plantron Computer GmbH	Bad Homburg	06172-25188	

CAN YOU *GET BY* ?

MEETING PEOPLE

1 a **2** Ich heiße . . . (*or* Mein Name ist . . .) **3** Wie heißen Sie, bitte? (*or* Wie ist Ihr Name, bitte?) **4** Danke, gut. **5** b **6** Ich hätte gern (*or* ich möchte) ein Kännchen Kaffee, eine Cola und ein Bier (, bitte). **7** b.

SHOPPING

8 d **9** Ich hätte gern (*or* ich möchte) ein Kilo Tomaten und drei Bananen (, bitte). **10** Was (*or* wieviel) kostet eine Postkarte nach Großbritannien, bitte?/0,60 DM (Ich möchte) bitte drei Briefmarken **11** dreihundertfünfzig **12** d.

FINDING SOMEWHERE TO STAY

13 c **14** c **15** a **16** Können Sie mir ein Taxi bestellen? (*or* Ich hätte gern ein Taxi.)/Siebenundneunzig.

GETTING ABOUT

17 c   **18** b   **19**   Entschuldigen Sie, wie komme ich am besten zur Pinakothek?   **20**   Wie weit ist das zu Fuß?
21   Und (wie weit ist das) mit dem Bus?   **22**   Wo ist die nächste Bushaltestelle?   **23** d.

EATING OUT

24   Herr Ober, die Speisekarte, bitte!   **25** i   **26** b   **27** c
28 f   **29** h   **30** k   **31**   Was würden Sie (denn heute) empfehlen?   **32**   Was ist das, bitte?   **33**   Das nehme ich.   **34** a   **35**   Herr Ober! Die Rechnung, bitte!
36   56,50 DM   **37** d   **38**   two 20 DM notes; one 2 DM coin; one 1 DM coin; one 50 pfennig coin   **39** b.

DOWN TO BUSINESS

40 c   **41**   930 06 405   **42** c   **43**   Mein Name ist . . . Ich komme aus London, (ich bin) von der Firma Joy Computers. Ich habe um elf Uhr einen Termin bei Herrn Fischer.
44   Ich bin Importleiter./Ich arbeite bei (der Firma) Joy Computers in London. Ja./Ich habe zwei Töchter und einen Sohn./Sie heißen Mary, Jane und Gordon./Mary ist drei, Jane ist sieben und Gordon ist elf (Jahre alt).

WORD LIST

Abbreviations: (*m.*) masculine, (*f.*) feminine, (*s.*) singular, (*pl.*) plural, (*refl.*) reflexive verb, (*sep.*) separable verbs, (*col.*) colloquial, (*lit.*) literally, (*s. Ger.*) south German. Plural forms of nouns are given in brackets.

The English meanings apply to the words as they are used in this book and *Get by in German Plus*.

A

à   per

die **Aalsuppe (-n)**   eel soup

der **Abend (-e)**   evening;
   guten Abend! good evening!
   das **Abendessen (-)**   dinner
   abends   in the evenings
   aber   but, also used for emphasis: **das ist aber nett**   that's very nice (of you)!
   abfahren (*sep.*)   to leave

die **Abfahrt (-en)**   departure
   abholen (*sep.*)   to meet, to pick up
   ach   oh

die **Adresse (-n)**   address
   AG = Aktiengesellschaft   plc

die **Allee (-n)**   avenue
   alles   all, everything; **das ist alles**   that's all
   als   as, for **also**   so
   alt   old

die **Altstadt (ー̈e)**   old part of town
   am = an dem   at/on the

am Donnerstag   on Thursday

andere   other; **ein anderes Land**   another country

die   **Ampel (-n)**   traffic light

anbieten (*sep.*)   to offer

der   **Anfang (¨e)**   beginning

der   *or* die **Angestellte (-n)**   employee, assistant

anmelden   to tell someone you're there

der   **Anruf (-e)**   telephone call

anrufen (*sep.*)   to call, to phone, to ring up

die   **Anschrift (-en)**   address

die   **Antwort (-en)**   answer

der   **Apfel(¨)**   apple

der   **Apfelstrudel (-)**   kind of apple turnover

die   **Apotheke (-n)**   pharmacy

der   **Appetit**   appetite; **guten Appetit!**   enjoy your meal!

die   **Arbeit (-en)**   work

arbeiten (bei)   to work (at)

der   **Arzt (¨e)**   doctor

die   **Ärztin (-nen)**   doctor (*f.*)

die   **Arzthelferin (-nen)**   doctor's assistant

auch   also, as well

auf   on, onto, at; **auf Wiedersehen!**   goodbye!; **auf Wiederhören!** goodbye! (on the phone)

der   **Aufschnitt**   sliced cold meats, sausage

aufstehen (*sep.*)   to get up; **wann stehen Sie auf?**   what time do you get up?

der   **Augenblick (-e)** = **der Moment(-e)**   moment

aus   out, out of, from

der   **Ausgang (¨e)**   exit, way out

ausgebucht   fully booked

ausgeschildert   signposted

ausgezeichnet   excellent

die   **Auskunft (¨e)**   directory enquiries

ausmachen (*sep.*)   to arrange

ausrichten (*sep.*)   to give someone a message

außerdem   besides;

außerdem noch etwas?   anything else?

ausverkauft   sold out

das **Auto (-s)** car
die **Autobahn (-en)** motorway
automatisch automatically

das **Bad (¨er)** bath
bald soon; **sobald wie möglich** as soon as possible
die **Bank (-en)** bank
der **Bahnhof (¨e)** railway station
die **Banane (-n)** banana
der **Barmann (¨er)** barman
Bayern Bavaria
der **Beamte (n)** clerk, official (*m.*)
die **Beamtin (-nen)** clerk, official (*f.*)
bedanken: ich bedanke mich thank you
bedienen to serve; **sich bedienen** to help oneself
bei (m) at (the)
das **Beispiel (-e)** example;
zum Beispiel for example
bekommen to get
das **Benzin** petrol
der **Beruf (-e)** job, profession
die **Besprechung (-en)** meeting
bestellen to order; **ich habe bestellt** I've ordered
besten: wie komme ich am besten? what's the best way to?
besuchen to visit
das **Bett (-en)** bed
bezahlen to pay
das **Bier (-e)** beer
bin: ich bin I am
bis until, till; **bis zum/zur** up to (the); **von . . . bis . . .** from . . . till . . .
bissl (*s. Ger.*) see **bißchen**
bißchen: ein bißchen a little/bit
bitte please; **bitte sehr,**
bitte schön don't mention it, (offering something) here you are; **bitte sehr?, bitte schön?** what can I do for you?, yes please
bitten to ask

blau blue
bleiben to stay
bleifrei lead free (petrol)
die **Bootsfahrt (-en)** boat trip
die **Bratkartoffel (-n)** fried potato
brauchen to need; **ich bräuchte** I need, please
braun brown
der **Brief (-e)** letter
die **Briefmarke (-n)** stamp
bringen to bring, serve
das **Brötchen (-)** bread roll
das **Brot (-e)** bread
die **Brücke (-n)** bridge
das **Büro (-s)** office
die **Bushaltestelle (-n)** busstop
die **Butter** butter

C

ca (= cirka) about
das **Café (-s)** café
der **Campingplatz (¨e)** camp site
der **Champignon (-s)** mushroom
der **Cocktail (-s)** cocktail
die **Cola (-s)** coke

D

da there; **den/die/das da** that one there; **da drüben** over there
dabei with you
die **Dame (-n)** lady, madam
Dank: herzlichen/schönen/vielen Dank! many thanks!; **danke,
danke schön, danke sehr** thank you; **nein, danke** no thank you
dann then
darf: darf es die sein? is this one all right? (*lit.* may it be this one?)
see **dürfen**
das this, that, the
die **Dauer** duration
dauern to last; **wie lange dauert die Fahrt?** how long does the

journey take?

dazu   with it, in addition

dem, den, der   the, this/that one

denn   for, because, then

das **Dessert (-s)**   dessert

deutsch   German

das **Deutschlernen**   the learning of German

die   the, that

diese, diesem, diesen, dieser   this, these

die **Dillkartoffel (-n)**   dill potato

direkt   direct(ly)

die **DM (D-Mark), Deutsche
Mark**   German currency

doch   yes (in answer to a negative question)

das **Doppelzimmer (-)**   double room

dort   there

die **Dose (-n)**   tin, can

drauf (short for **darauf**)   on it; **das kommt drauf an**   it depends (on)

dreimal   three times, three (of)

dritte   third

die **Drogerie (-n)**   chemist's

drüben, da drüben   over there

durch   through

durchstellen (*sep.*) = **verbinden**   to connect, put through

die **Durchwahl(nummer) (-n)**   direct telephone number

dürfen   to be allowed; **darf ich?**   may I?; **dürfte ich?**   might/could I?

die **Dusche (-n)**   shower

<table><tr><td>E</td></tr></table>

der **Edamer**   Edam cheese

die **Ecke (-n)**   corner

das **Ei (-er)**   egg

ein, eine, einen, einer, einem   a, one

einbiegen (*sep.*)   to turn into

einfach   simple, simply; **einfache Fahrt**   single journey

einkaufen (*sep.*)   to go shopping

einlösen   to cash

einmal   once, one (ticket)

einsteigen (*sep.*)   to board
eintragen (*sep.*): **sich eintragen**   to register, put your name down
das **Einzelzimmer (-)**   single room
das **Eis**   ice, ice cream
der **Elbtunnel (-)**   Elbe tunnel
der **Empfang (¨-e)**   reception
die **Empfangsdame (-n)**   receptionist (*f*)
empfehlen   to recommend
das **Ende (-n)**   end
der **Engländer (-)**   English(man)
die **Engländerin (-nen)**   English(woman)
entlang   along
entschuldigen: entschuldigen Sie! entschuldigung!   excuse me
erste, erster   first; **erstmal** first of all
der **Erwachsene (-n)**   adult
es   it
das **Essen (-)**   meal
essen   to eat
die **Etage (-n)**   storey, floor
etwa   about
etwas   something; **noch etwas?** anything else?
der **Exportleiter (-)**   export manager (*m.*)
die **Exportleiterin (-nen)**   export manager (*f.*)
extra   special, additional

F

fahren   to drive, go (by transport), travel
das **Fahrrad (¨-er)**   bicycle
die **Fahrt (-en)**   trip
fährt ab   leaves
das **Fahrzeug (-e)**   vehicle
die **Familie (-n)**   family
die **Farbe (-n)**   colour
fein   fine
das **Fenster (-)**   window
die **Ferien** (*pl.*)   holidays, vacation
fertigmachen (*sep.*)   to prepare

das **Filet (-s)** fillet
finden to find
die **Firma (Firmen)** company
der **Fisch (-e)** fish
die **Flasche (-n)** bottle
das **Fleisch** meat
der **Flughafen (-)** airport
fönen to blow dry
die **Frage (-n)** question
das **Fräulein (-)** Miss
der **Frankenwein (-e)** Franconian wine
die **Frau (-en)** woman; **Frau Peters** Mrs Peters
frei free; **haben Sie ein Zimmer frei?** have you got a room available?
fremd strange; **ich bin hier fremd** I'm a stranger here
die **Freesie (-n)** freesia
der **Freund (-e)** friend
frisch fresh
der **Friseur (-e)** hairdresser, barber
früh early; **morgen früh** tomorrow morning
das **Frühstück (-e)** breakfast
frühstücken to have breakfast
das **Frühstücksbüffet (-s)** breakfast buffet
für for
der **Fuß (-e)** foot; **zu Fuß** on foot
die **Fußgängerpassage (-n)** pedestrian underpass

G

ganz quite
der **Garten (-)** garden
der **Gast (-e)** guest
die **Gaststätte (-n)** pub, inn
das **Gebäude (-)** building
geben to give
gebraten fried
gefällt: gefällt es Ihnen? do you like it?
gegen . . . Uhr at about . . . o'clock

gehen to go, walk; **es geht** not too bad; **das geht** that's possible; **wann geht die nächste . . .?** when is the next . . .?

gekocht, gekochten cooked

gelb yellow

das **Gemüse** vegetables

genug enough

geöffnet open

gerade just

das **Gepäck** luggage

geradeaus straight on, straight ahead

gern, gerne gladly; yes please, fine

geschmeckt: hat es Ihnen geschmeckt? did you enjoy it?

geschnitten sliced

gestern yesterday

gesund healthy

die **Getränkekarte (-n)** drinks menu

gewählt chosen

gibt: gibt es? is there?

ginge: das ginge that would be possible

das **Glas (¨er)** glass

glauben to think

gleich in a minute, just; **gleich hier vorne** just in front here

gleichfalls the same to you

das **Gleis (-e)** platform

GmbH = Gesellschaft mit beschränkter Haftung Ltd

der **Gott (¨er)** god

das **Gramm (-e)** gram

der **Grill (-s)** grill

groß, großen, großer, großes large, big

Großbritannien Great Britain

grün green

grüß: grüß Gott! (*s. Ger.*) greeting

die **Gulaschsuppe (-n)** goulash soup

gut, gute, guten good, fine, well

gute Nacht! good night!;

guten Abend! good evening!; **guten Morgen!** good morning!;

guten Tag! good day!

H

der	**Haarschnitt (-e)**	hairdo, haircut

der Haarschnitt (-e) hairdo, haircut

haben to have

hatte: ich hatte I had

hätte: ich hätte gern(e) . . . I'd like . . .; **was hätten Sie gern(e)?** what would you like?

die **Hafenrundfahrt (-en)** trip round the harbour

halb, halbes half; **halb fünf** half past four; **ein halbes Pfund** half a pound, 250 grams

hallo! hello!

halten, sich halten (*refl.*) to keep (to); **halten Sie sich rechts** keep to the right

der **Hauptbahnhof (¨e)** main railway station

der **Hauptgang (¨e) = das Hauptgericht (-e)** main course

das **Haus (¨er)** house; **nach Hause** (to) home

das **Heilbuttsteak (-s)** halibut steak

heiß hot

heißen to be called; **ich heiße** my name is; **wie heißen Sie?** what's your name?

helfen to help

herein in

der **Herr (-en)** sir, gentleman;

Herr Meier Mr Meier

die **Herrschaften** (*pl.*) ladies and gentlemen

herzlich hearty; **herzlich willkommen!** you're very welcome!

heute today

hier here

die **Himbeertorte (-n)** raspberry flan

hinein in, into

hin und zurück return, (*lit.* there and back)

hinüber across

hinunter down

historisch historical

hoch up

das **Hochhaus (-ër)** skyscraper

der **Holländer (Käse)** Dutch (cheese)

holländisch Dutch

das **Hotel (-s)** hotel

hübsch pretty

I

ich I
ihn him, it
Ihnen (to) you
Ihr, Ihre, Ihren, Ihrem, Ihrer your
im = in dem in (the)
immer always
in in
in Ordnung all right, OK
der **Ingenieur (-e)** engineer
die **Innenstadt (¨e)** city centre
die **Insel (-n)** island
ist is
Italien Italy

J

ja yes
das **Jägerschnitzel (-)** pork escalope 'hunter style' (in chasseur sauce)
das **Jahr (-e)** year

K

der **Kaffee (-s)** coffee
kann can; **was kann ich für Sie tun?** what can I do for you?
das **Kännchen (-)** small pot
die **Kantine (-n)** canteen
der **Käse (-)** cheese
das **Käseomelett (-e** or **-s)** cheese omelette
die **Kasse (-n)** cash desk
der **Kassierer (-)** cashier
die **Karte (-n)** card, postcard, ticket
kaufen to buy
kein, keine, keinen, keinem, keiner no, not any
der **Keks (-e)** biscuit
der **Keller (-)** cellar
der **Kellner (-)** waiter

die **Kellnerin (-nen)** waitress
das **Kilo(gramm)** kilo(gram)
der **Kilometer** kilometre
das **Kind (-er)** child
die **Kirche (-n)** church
die **Klasse (-n)** class
   klein, kleinen, kleiner, kleines small
das **Kleingeld** small change
   klingen to sound; **das klingt gut** that sounds good
der **Knoblauch** garlic
   Köln Cologne
   kombiniert combined
das **Komma (-ta** *or* **-s)** comma
die **Konditorei (-en)** café, patisserie
   kommen (aus) to come (from)
die **Konferenz (-en)** conference, meeting
   können to be able; **können Sie?** can you?
der **Kopfsalat (-e)** lettuce
   kosten to cost
die **Krabbe (-n)** prawn
die **Krabbensuppe (-n)** prawn soup
die **Krebssuppe (-n)** crayfish soup
die **Kreditkarte (-n)** credit card
der **Kuchen (-)** cake
der **Kuchenbon (-s)** cake ticket
der **Kunde (-n)** customer (*m.*)
die **Kundin (-nen)** customer (*f.*)
die **Kunsthalle (-n)** art gallery
das **Kunstmuseum (-museen)** art museum
der **Kurze (-n)** 'short'
die **Kutterscholle (-n)** type of large plaice

L

das **Labskaus** Hamburg sailor's dish
das **Land (ᵘer)** country
   lang long; **wie lange?** how long?
der **Leberwurst (ᵘe)** liver sausage

der **Lehrer (-)** teacher (*m.*)
die **Lehrerin (-nen)** teacher (*f.*)
lieber rather, preferably
leid: (das) tut mir leid I'm sorry
leider unfortunately
liegen to be situated, lie
links (on, to the) left; **auf der linken Seite** on the left-hand side
der *or* das **Liter (-)** litre

M

machen to make, do; **wird gemacht!** right away!; **was macht das?** how much is it?
das **Mädchen (-)** girl
das **Mal (-e)** time(s); **das vierte Mal** the fourth time
Mallorca Majorca
man one; **wo kann man?** where can one?
manchmal sometimes
der **Mann (-̈er)** man
die **Mark (-)** mark (German currency)
die **Marmelade (-n)** jam
mehr more
mehrere several
mein, meine, meiner my
meistens mostly
der *or* das **Meter (-)** metre
das **Menü (-s)** set-price meal
mich me
die **Milch** milk
die **Million (-en)** million
das **Mineralwasser (-̈)** mineral water
die **Minibar (-s)** minibar
die **Minute (-n)** minute
mir (to) me
mit with; **mit dem Bus** by bus
mitreisen (*sep.*) to join the trip
das **Mittagessen (-)** lunch
die **Mittagspause (-n)** lunch

die **Mitte (-n)** middle; **Mitte März** mid March
möchte: ich möchte I'd like
möchten: wir möchten we'd like; **möchten Sie . . .?** would you
like . . . ?
mögen to like
möglich possible
die **Mokkatorte (-n)** coffee gateau
der **Moment (-e)** moment;
einen Moment, bitte just a moment, please
der **Monat (-e)** month
der **Morgen (-)** morning;
guten Morgen! good morning! **morgen** tomorrow; **morgen früh**
tomorrow morning
die **Mosel** (river) Moselle; **der Moselwein** Moselle wine
München Munich
muß: ich muß I must/have to
müssen to have to

N

nach: Viertel nach acht quarter past eight; **nach Bremen** to Bremen
der **Nachmittag (-e)** afternoon
nachmittags in the afternoons
nachsehen (*sep.*) to check
die **Nacht (-̈e)** night; **gute Nacht!** good night
der, **die, das nächste** nearest, next
die **Nähe: hier in der Nähe** near here, nearby, in the vicinity
der **Name (-n)** name
natürlich of course
nebenan nearby, right
here (*lit.* next door)
nee (*col.*) see **nein**
nehmen to take; **ich
nehme Tee** I'll have tea
nein no; **nein, danke** no, thank you
nett nice
neu new
nicht not
nichts nothing

noch also, still: **auch noch** as well; **noch etwas?** anything else?;
noch zwei Bier two more beers
nochmal again
die **Nordsee** North Sea
normalerweise usually
Norwegen Norway
die **Nummer (-n)** number
nur only
die **Nußtorte (-n)** nut gateau

<hr>

O

der **Ober (-)** waiter
oder or
die **Öffnungszeiten** (*pl.*) opening hours
oft often
ohne without
die **Oma (-s)** grandma
der **Orangensaft (¨e)** orange juice
Ordnung: in Ordnung! OK!, fine (*lit.* in order)
organisieren to organise
der **Ort (-e)** place
ost east

<hr>

P

paar: ein paar a few
das **Paket (-e)** packet
das **Papiertaschentuch (¨er)** paper tissue
der **Park (-s)** park
parken to park
das **Parkhaus (¨er)** multi-storey car park
der **Passagier (-e)** passenger
der **Passant (-en)** passer-by (*m.*)
der **Paß (-ässe)** passport
paßt: was paßt? what fits/suits?
der **Patient (-en)** patient (*m.*)
die **Patientin (-nen)** patient (*f.*)
die **Person (-en)** person

der **Personalchef (-s)** personnel manager
der **Personenzug (-̈e)** slow local train
die **Petersilie** parsley
der **Pfennig (-e)** pfennig (German currency)
der **Pfirsich (-e)** peach
die **Pfirsichtorte (-n)** peach flan
der **Pförtner (-)** porter
das **Pfund (-e)** pound, half a kilo
der **Pinguin (-e)** penguin
der **PKW (Personenkraftwagen) (-)** car
der **Plan (-̈e)** map, plan;
   Großer Plan name of street in Celle
der **Platz (-̈e)** seat, place, space
der **Platzwart (-e)** campsite warden
der **Polizist (-en)** policeman
die **Pommes frites** (pl.) chips
die **Post** post office
das **Postamt (-̈er)** post office
die **Postkarte (-n)** postcard
   pro per
der **Produktmanager (-)** product manager
das **Produktmeeting (-s)** product meeting
   prost! cheers

R

die **Rechnung (-en)** bill
   recht correct, right
   rechts (on, to the) right; **auf der rechten Seite** on the right-hand side
die **Regel (-n)** rule; **in der Regel** as a rule
   reif ripe
   rein: kommen Sie rein come in
die **Reise (-n)** journey, trip
der **Reisescheck (-s)** traveller's cheque
   reservieren to book
das **Restaurant (-s)** restaurant
der **Rheinwein (-e)** Rhine wine
die **Rose (-n)** rose
   rot red

der **Rotwein (-e)** red wine
der **Ruhetag (-e)** rest day
das **Rumpsteak (-s)** rump steak
runter (short for **herunter**) down here

S

sagen to say
die **Sahne** cream
das **Sahnesteak (-s)** steak with cream sauce
der **Salat (-e)** salad
das **Sanatorium (-ien)** sanatorium
die **Sardine (-n)** sardine
schade! what a pity!
das **Schauspielhaus (-̈er)** theatre, playhouse
das **Schild (-er)** sign
der **Schinken (-)** ham
schlecht bad
das **Schloß (-̈sser)** castle
der **Schlüssel (-)** key
schmecken to taste; **hat es Ihnen geschmeckt?** did you enjoy it?
der **Schnaps (-̈e)** schnaps
schneiden to cut, slice; **geschnitten** sliced
schnell quick(ly); **wie komme ich am schnellsten?** what's the
quickest way?
die **Schnellbahn = S-Bahn (-en)** fast local train system
das **Schnitzel (-)** escalope
die **Schokolade (-n)** (hot) chocolate
die **Scholle (-n)** plaice
schon already
schön nice, lovely, beautiful; **bitte schön?** yes, please?; **bitte schön!**
not at all!
schönen Dank! many thanks!
der **Schotte (-n)** Scot(sman)
die **Schottin (-nen)** Scot(swoman)
schreiben to write
das **Schwarzbrot (-e)** (black) rye bread
die **Schwarzwälder Kirschtorte (-n)** 'Black Forest' cherry gateau
schwierig difficult

sehen   to see

sehr   very; **bitte sehr!**   not at all!

sein   to be

die **Seite (-n)**   side; **auf der rechten/linken Seite**   on the right/left-hand side

das **Sekretariat (-e)**   secretariat

die **Sekretärin (-nen)**   secretary (f.)

selbst tanken   to serve oneself with petrol

das **Seminar (-e)**   seminar

der **Senatorentopf**   meat and vegetable dish

sich   oneself, yourself

sicher(lich)   sure(ly), certain(ly)

sie   they, she, it

Sie   you (formal)

sind: Sie/wir/sie sind   you/we/they are

der **Skat**   card game

so   so; **so . . . wie . . .**   as . . . as . . .

sofort   straightaway

der **Sohn (⁻e)**   son

sollen   to be supposed to; **sollte: sollte ich?**   should I?

sonnabends   on Saturdays

die **Sonne (-n)**   sun

sonst: sonst noch etwas?   anything else?

sonntags   on Sundays

die **Sorte (-n)**   sort, kind, type

Spanien   Spain

der **Spaß (⁻e)**   joke, fun; **viel Spaß!**   have fun

spät   late

spazierengehen (sep.)   to go for a walk

die **Speisekarte (-n)**   menu

spielen   to play

speisen   to eat, dine

sprechen   to speak

der **Stadtplan (⁻e)**   city map

die **Stadtrundfahrt (-en)**   city sightseeing tour

der **Statistiker (-)**   statistician (m.)

stehen   to stand, to be

stellen   to put

stimmt: das stimmt so that's all right
die **Straße (-n)** street
die **Straßenbahn (-en)** tram
das **Stück (-e)** piece (of), item
die **Stunde (-n)** hour
der **Süden** south
das **Super** 4-star petrol
der **Supermarkt (⁻e)** supermarket

T

der **Tag (-e)** day; **guten Tag!** *lit.* good day!
die **Tagessuppe (-n)** soup of the day
täglich daily
die **Tagung (-en)** meeting, conference
der **Tankwart (-e)** petrol pump attendant
die **Tasche (-n)** pocket
die **Tasse (-n)** cup
die **Taxe (-n)** or das **Taxi (-s)** taxi
der **Taxifahrer (-)** taxi-driver (*m.*)
die **Taxifahrerin (-nen)** taxi-driver (*f.*)
der **Tee (-s)** tea
die **Teewurst (⁻e)** type of sausage
telefonieren to telephone
die **Telefonnummer (-n)** telephone number
die **Telefonzelle (-n)** telephone box
das **Tennis** tennis
der **Termin (-e)** appointment
der **Terminkalender (-)** diary
der **Tisch (-e)** table
die **Tochter (⁻)** daughter
die **Toilette (-n)** toilet
die **Tomate (-n)** tomato
der **Topf (⁻e)** pot
der **Tourist (-en)** tourist (*m.*)
traditionell traditional
die **Traube (-n)** grape
treffen to meet; **sich treffen** (refl.): **wo treffen wir uns?** where
shall we meet?

die **Treppe (-n)** steps, staircase
trinken to drink
trocken dry
tschüs! (*col.*) cheers, cheerio, 'bye!
tun to do; **was kann ich für Sie tun?** what can I do for you?

U

die **U-Bahn Station (-en)** underground station
über across, over, via
überlegen to think
Uhr: wieviel Uhr ist es? what time is it?
um at; **um . . . Uhr** at . . . o'clock; **um die Ecke** round the corner
umsteigen (*sep.*) to change (train, tram, bus)
und and
ungarisch Hungarian
ungefähr about
uns (to) us
unten down below
unterschreiben to sign
die **Unterschrift (-en)** signature
der **Urlaub (-e)** holiday
usw = und so weiter and so on, etc.

V

das **Vanille-Eis** vanilla ice cream
die **Veranstaltung (-en)** event
verbinden to connect
verfügung: zur verfügung available
verheiratet married
der **Verkäufer (-)** shop assistant, stallholder (*m.*)
die **Verkäuferin (-nen)** shop assistant, stallholder (*f.*)
verschieden different
der **Vertreter (-)** representative (*m.*)
die **Vertreterin (-nen)** representative (*f.*)
der **Verwalter (-)** manager
viel much, a lot
viele many; **vielen Dank!** many thanks

    vielleicht perhaps
    viermal four times, four (of)
    vierte fourth
das **Viertel (-)** quarter
    voll full up
    volltanken (*sep.*) to fill up (with petrol)
    von of, from
    vor to, in front of, before
    vorab to start with
der **Vormittag (-e)** morning
    vormittags in the morning(s)
    vorn(e) in front
der **Vorname (-n)** first name
die **Vorspeise (-n)** starter
    vorstellen to introduce
die **Vorwahl(nummer) (-n)** dialling code

W

    wählen to choose
    war, wäre, waren was, would be
    wann? when?
    was für . . . ? what kind of . . .?
    was? what? **was hätten Sie gerne?** what would you like?
    waschen to wash
das **Wasser (-)** water
der **Wattwagen (-)** horse-drawn cart used to cross mud flats
    wechselhaft changeable
    wegen for, because of
    wegfahren (*sep.*) to go away; **fahren Sie weg?** do you go away?
    weichgekochtes: ein weichgekochtes Ei a soft-boiled egg
der **Wein (-e)** wine
die **Weinkarte (-n)** wine list
die **Weintraube (-n)** grape
    weiß white
der **Weißwein (-e)** white wine
    weit far
    weiter (further) on

welcher?, welche?, welchem? which?

wenn if, when; **wenn es geht** if possible

die **Werbeabteilung(en)** publicity department

der **West (-en)** west

das **Wetter** weather

der **Widerwille** reluctance, disgust

wie? how? what? **wie geht's?** how are you?; **wie komme ich . . . ?** how do I get . . . ?

wie lange? how long?

wieder again

Wiederhören: auf Wiederhören! goodbye! (on the phone)

Wiedersehen: auf Wiedersehen! goodbye!

wieviel? how much?; **wie viele?** how many?

willkommen welcome

der **Winter** winter

wir we

der **Wirt (-e)** landlord, pub owner

wo? where?; **wo gibt es . . . ?** where is there . . . ?

woandershin (to go) somewhere different

die **Woche (-n)** week

das **Wochenende (-n)** weekend

woher? where from?

wohin? where (to)?

Wohl: zum Wohl! cheers!, your health!

wohnen to live

der **Wohnwagen (-)** caravan

wollen to wish, want; **wollen Sie mit?** do you want to join us?

wunderbar wonderful

der **Wunsch (-̈e)** wish

würden: ich würde gern (e) I'd like; **würden Sie?** would you?

die **Wurst (-̈e)** sausage

Z

der **Zahnarzt (-̈e)** dentist (*m.*)

zeigen to show; **das kann ich Ihnen zeigen** I can show you that

das **Zelt (-e)** tent

die **Zeitung (-en)** newspaper

der **Zeltplatz (¨e)**   camp site; tent pitch

ziemlich   fairly, rather

das **Zimmer (-)**   room

der **Zimmerausweis (-e)**   room card

die **Zimmernummer (-n)**   room number

der **Zimmerschlüssel (-)**   room key

zirka   about

die **Zitrone (-n)**   lemon

die **Zitronenbutter**   lemon butter

das **Zitronensorbet (-s)**   lemon sorbet

zu   to; **zu Ende**   over; **zu Fuß**   on foot; **zu sechzig** at sixty

der **Zug (¨e)**   train

zur Verfügung   available

zum (= zu dem), zur (= zu der)   to the

zurück   back; **hin und zurück**   there and back, return (ticket)

zusammen   together

zweimal   twice, two (of)

das **Zweipersonenzelt (-e)**   two-person tent

zweite   second

zwo = zwei   two

zwomal see **zweimal**